teach®
yourself

basic computer skills

moira stephen

for over 60 years, more than 40
million people have learnt over
750 subjects the **teach yourself**
way, with impressive results.

be where you want to be with
teach yourself

For UK orders: please contact Bookpoint Ltd, 130 Milton Park, Abingdon, Oxon OX14 4SB. Telephone: +44 (0)/1235 827720. Fax: +44 (0)/1235 400454. Lines are open 09.00–18.00, Monday to Saturday, with a 24-hour message answering service. Details about our titles and how to order are available at www.teachyourself.co.uk

For USA order enquiries: please contact McGraw-Hill Customer Services, PO Box 545, Blacklick, OH 43004-0545, USA. Telephone: 1-800-722-4726. Fax: 1-614-755-5645.

For Canada order enquiries: please contact McGraw-Hill Ryerson Ltd, 300 Water St, Whitby, Ontario L1N 9B6, Canada. Telephone: 905 430 5000. Fax: 905 430 5020.

Long renowned as the authoritative source for self-guided learning – with more than 30 million copies sold worldwide – the *Teach Yourself* series includes over 300 titles in the fields of languages, crafts, hobbies, business, computing and education.

British Library Cataloguing in Publication Data
A catalogue record for this title is available from The British Library.

Library of Congress Catalog Card Number: On file.

First published in UK 2003 by Hodder Headline Plc, 338 Euston Road, London, NW1 3BH.

First published in US 2003 by Contemporary Books, A Division of The McGraw-Hill Companies, 1 Prudential Plaza, 130 East Randolph Street, Chicago, Illinois 60601 USA.

The 'Teach Yourself' name is a registered trade mark of Hodder & Stoughton Ltd.
Computer hardware and software brand names mentioned in this book are protected by their respective trademarks and are acknowledged.

Copyright © 2003 Moira Stephen

Typeset by MacDesign, Southampton
Printed in Great Britain for Hodder & Stoughton Educational, a division of Hodder Headline Plc, 338 Euston Road, London NW1 3BH by Cox & Wyman Ltd, Reading, Berkshire.

Impression number   10 9 8 7 6 5 4 3 2 1
Year   2007 2006 2005 2004 2003

contents

preface

Teach Yourself Basic Computer Skills is for anyone who wants to learn how to make good use of their PC. It doesn't assume that you are a complete novice – there are very few of those left! You have sat at a keyboard and done a little with one application perhaps, and now want to get to grips with more. You may even be thinking of taking a basic qualification in IT. This book will get you off to a good start with Word, Excel, Access, PowerPoint, the Internet and e-mail.

The book starts by looking at the world of ICT (Information and Communications Technology). You are introduced to the jargon, PCs in the home, education and work, legal considerations and e-commerce.

Chapter 2 goes on to help you get started *using* your PC and working in Windows. You will be taken from switching on, through customizing your desktop, using the on-line help, managing your folders and files and installing software.

Chapter 3 covers features that are pretty standard across all of the Microsoft Office applications, such as creating, saving, printing, closing and opening files. Other topics include basic formatting options, moving and copying text and data, spell checking, searching, clip art and drawing.

Word is introduced in Chapter 4. You will learn how to create and manipulate basic documents, format using tabs and indents, create and edit tables, use styles and templates, perform a mail merge and create and format graphs.

In Chapter 5 you will find out how to unleash the power of Excel. As you create and format your worksheets, you will find out how to build formulas, use functions and create and format graphs.

The Access database package is introduced in Chapter 6. You will learn how to create tables and input and edit data. You will also find out how to create forms and use them for data input, manipulate your data by sorting and querying it, and present your data effectively using reports.

Chapter 7 will teach you how to create effective presentations using Microsoft PowerPoint. You will find out how to add text, tables, pictures, charts and other objects to your slides. You will also learn how to add special effects and present the finished product.

Finally, Chapter 8 introduces you to the Internet and e-mail. You will learn how to locate web sites, surf the net, customize your browser and manage your favorites. You will also find out how to send and reply to e-mails, sent attachments and manage your messages.

I hope you enjoy *Teach Yourself Basic Computer Skills*, and make good use of your new skills.

Moira Stephen
2003

01

information and communications technology

In this chapter you will learn

- what ICT is about
- how computers are used at work and at home
- some essential computer jargon

1.1 A brief history lesson

Some of the theories and ideas that would eventually come together to help make up the modern computer were conceived back in the 19th century.

In the 1830s, Charles Babbage (an English inventor) invented several mechanical calculating machines. His Analytical Engine (although never actually built) was designed to perform some of the tasks digital computers perform today, e.g. store instructions, perform calculations and have a permanent memory (punched cards would have been used). Had it been built it would have been huge – covering an area about the size of a football pitch!

In the 1840s, George Boole devised a system of mathematics which became known as Boolean Algebra. The system used binary (true/false) logic and is central to how computers made decisions.

By the end of the century analogue computers appeared. Herman Hollerith (a US inventor) patented a calculating machine. It used punched cards and in 1890 it was used to compute census data.

It was during the 20th century that the major developments leading to our modern computers took place.

In the first quarter of the century Hollerith's Tabulating Machine Company experienced several mergers. In 1924 it was finally absorbed into a company which adopted the name International Business Machines Corporation (IBM).

The Second World War provided a huge stimulus to computer development. Howard Aiken (an American) led the development of a computer known as the Mark 1. It was used by the naval artillery. The British developed a computer to decode messages from the German Enigma machine.

Shortly after the war the Americans built the ENIAC – the most sophisticated computer of its time.

In 1947 Bell Laboratories in the USA invented the transistor. A few years later the microchip and microprocessor were invented. These could store and manipulate information in a small space.

In 1974 Micro Instrumentation Telemetry Systems, in New Mexico, released the Altair 8800 – the first personal computer.

In 1975 the Microsoft Corporation was founded by William H. Gates III (Bill Gates) and Paul Allen. They collaborated on the first version of the BASIC programming language for the MITS Altair. They moved Microsoft to a suburb of their home town of Seattle, Washington in 1979. Two years later they took their first step in diversifying beyond programming languages when they released MS-DOS, the operating system for the original IBM PC. Microsoft went on to convince other PC manufacturers to license MS-DOS, which made it the de facto software standard for PCs.

Microsoft moved into application software, e.g. Word and Excel, and extended beyond the PC. In 1984 they began to produce application software for the Apple Macintosh.

The 1970s and early 1980s saw the development of ARPAnet, a long-distance computer network devised by the US Government's Advanced Research Projects Agency and its evolution into the first stages of what is now the Internet. From an initial network of four computers, another 200 in military and research establishments throughout the USA were linked using this network during the 1970s. By the mid-1980s several academic networks had also been set up. These combined with the ARPAnet to form the Internet.

Computers became progressively smaller, better and cheaper in the 1980s, and by 1992 the computer industry was the fastest-growing industry in the world.

1991 saw the end of a decade of collaboration between Microsoft and IBM. IBM chose to pursue a former joint venture with Microsoft on the OS/2 operating system, while Microsoft chose to evolve its Windows operating system, delivering Windows 3.1 in 1992. There was further development of the Windows operating system through the 1990s and by the end of the century Microsoft had cornered the lion's share of the PC software market with Windows, its desktop applications and Internet browser.

1.2 Computers in everyday life

Where would we be without our computer? They are everywhere! They guide aircraft, control traffic, process words and numbers, store medical and dental records, and keep track of appointments – not to mention store your photographs and play your videos and music! You can use them to book your holidays, buy your wine, do your banking or research your favourite hobby. They have become the heart of modern business, research, and indeed everyday life.

Can you think of any area of your life that isn't influenced by the use of computers? Most of us find ourselves surrounded by them – and we're bound to become even more dependent on them as this century progresses.

At home

Many homes have computers and the number is on the increase. Most home computers are *multimedia* systems that can be used for work and play. A multimedia system can run application software (e.g. word processing, spreadsheet, desktop publishing), play music and video, run games software, and access the Internet, etc.

The home computer can be used in a variety of ways:

- Word processing software is used for letters, reports, invitations, lists, etc. Spreadsheets can be used for budgeting and managing the home accounts.

- School pupils and students find a home PC useful for homework and research. Encyclopaedias are available on CD and the Internet gives access to information on any subject.

- Internet access on a home PC also means that you can do home banking (if your bank provides the facility) and electronic mail (e-mail). You could also study a course on-line.

- Computer games are also popular on home PCs (games can also be played via the Internet).

- Home shopping is on the increase – many high street retail outlets have web sites and specialist Internet retailers, e.g. Amazon.com, have emerged.

- The number of people working from home has increased as many jobs that traditionally had to be done in the office can be carried out successfully on a home PC with Internet access. This *home working* is also referred to as *teleworking*. The benefits of home working are that it is flexible (you don't need to stick to the 9 to 5 routine), and you don't need to join the commuter trail to and from the office each day. However, some home workers feel isolated as they miss the social interaction of a central office, and it may be difficult to feel part of a team when working remotely.

At work and in education

Almost every organization depends on its computer system to manage its information and communicate with customers and other companies. Typical office applications software includes:

Word processing	for letters, reports, minutes, memos, etc.
Spreadsheet	for budgets, sales figures, anything involving calculations
Database	for customer records, supplier information, product information, personnel records
Presentation	for meetings, lectures, conferences
Information management	can be used for electronic diaries and organizers
Accounts	to keep tabs on purchases and sales
Desktop publishing	for company newsletters, leaflets

In addition to the packages above, specialized business environments may use applications specific to their work, e.g. graphic design or photographic image manipulation packages.

In industry, computers are used to control production lines and the manufacturing process and to manage stock control.

Computer assisted design and computer assisted manufacturing (CAD/CAM) is a process where software is used to design components on screen, then use the design information to control the machine that manufactures the component.

Government agencies use computers to store health records, housing information, social security records, criminal records, etc.

Educational establishments use applications in the classroom that are similar to those found in industry, e.g. the Microsoft Office suite to familiarize pupils with the type of software they will meet later in life. The administration requirements of educational establishments mean that typical business applications as found in the Office suite are usually required e.g. database for student records, word processing for reports/teaching materials, etc.

Computer Based Training (CBT) is a popular training method. Students can use the software to learn at their own pace, and repeat sections that they haven't quite grasped. Computerized exercises and games can be used to help reinforce the learning process. CBT packages are available for all ages and situations – they may be used to help toddlers to count, or to teach medical students about the body, or to train pilots to fly aeroplanes.

Companies may find CBT a cost-effective way to train staff – a package can be used many times for different staff (or the same member of staff over again). A possible disadvantage of CBT is that you don't have a tutor to ask when you don't understand something, and you may be working on your own, so you can't compare notes or discuss problems with your peers.

Many courses can also be studied over the Internet. This is referred to as *on-line learning*. Your notes and exercises will be available on the Web, you will be able to contact your tutor via e-mail, and you may be able to take part in 'discussion groups' with other students studying the same course over the Internet.

Computers are particularly useful when:

* Performing repetitive tasks
* Doing fast and accurate calculations
* Manipulating data
* Extracting data from different sources.

There are times however when the human touch is better. Many people would rather speak to someone if they have a query than try to extract data from a computer. People are also better at dealing with one-off situations – computers can't use their initiative or react to situations that they are not programmed to deal with.

Computers in daily life

Computers play a huge role in our daily life. Areas that you'll find them in include:

* Bill generation and management – gas, electricity, water, telephone, etc. billing systems are all computerized. The person who comes to read your meter may be carrying a computer!

* Airline booking, on-line banking, insurance claims processing are all done using computers.

* Money – Automatic Teller Machines (ATMs), or debit and credit cards use computers to record transactions.

* Vehicle registration records (at DVLC in the UK), census data and electronic voting are all managed on computer.

- Medical records – many doctors and dentists keep patient records on computer. Diagnostic tools, ambulance control systems and specialist surgical equipment may also be computer controlled.

- Supermarkets – barcode readers identify the product bought and the price is located on computer, the stock records are adjusted to reflect the sale.

- Libraries – electronic tagging facilitates computerized records of when books are issued and when they should be returned.

- Smart cards – cards with a microchip that contains a considerable amount of information about the holder could be used as combined debit/credit cards, identity cards, driving licence, emergency medical details, etc. Still relatively new, their use is likely to increase in the future.

1.3 Computer talk

This section introduces different types of computers and the main parts of a PC – input, output, processor and peripheral devices.

Types of computer

Personal Computer (PC)

The type of computer that you are most likely to use is the PC. Originally the PC was developed and marketed by IBM. Launched in 1981 it was such a success, that other companies copied it and marketed their own PC 'clone' as an IBM compatible PC.

The PC consists of a monitor, keyboard, mouse and a box containing the electronics, hard drive, memory, etc. The box may be under the monitor (in a desktop model), or it may stand beside it or on the floor under it (if the box is a tower model).

Laptop

As people began to rely more on their PC for business and personal use, the demand for a portable PC grew. This led to the development of laptops – smaller PCs powered by batteries that could be carried about in a briefcase. As the PCs were battery powered they would only work for a few hours before they had to be recharged – which meant you might need to take the charger with you (and perhaps a spare battery). Portable printers were designed so that you could print out your work while you were out and about, and, if you wanted to send/receive data and faxes, a cellular phone (connected to your laptop using an interface card and cable) could be used. A large briefcase is needed to carry all this hardware – useful, but perhaps a less portable solution than it first appears.

Hand-held devices/Palmtops

These PCs are small enough to be held in the palm of your hand. They use scaled-down versions of desktop software. They are very popular at a professional and personal level.

The **Personal Digital Assistant** (PDA) is a type of hand-held computer for personal and professional use. Originally designed as electronic organizers, they have developed into powerful devices. You can buy PDAs from many high street stores. Standard features that you would expect on a PDA are:

* **Personal information management** (**PIM**). Used to store contact information (names, addresses, phone numbers, e-mail addresses); compile task or to-do lists; take notes; write memos; keep track of appointments; remind you of appointments; (clock, alarm functions); plan projects; do calculations; keep track of expenses.

* Some of the more sophisticated models may be able to send or receive e-mail; do word processing; play MP3 music files and/or MPEG movie files; access the Internet; play video games; integrate things such as digital cameras and GPS receivers (global positioning systems used for navigation).

You can easily transfer data from your office or home PC onto your PDA, so they are very popular with people on the move, e.g. doctors, sales people, pilots, etc.

Network computers

You can use your PC as a stand-alone computer, or you can link it to others to form a network. Networks are discussed in more detail in section 1.7.

Mainframe and minicomputers

Mainframes and minicomputers are much bigger than PCs (although PCs may be connected to them via a network). These computers can store and process data for a whole organization.

Banks, insurance companies and retail stores will often use mainframes. Smaller organizations may be able to get by using a minicomputer.

Data input terminals

These may *look* like computers, but are actually input devices for the computer proper. You may have seen a data input terminal in action at the checkout of your local supermarket where the barcode reader scans the item purchased and enters the data into the central computer. The central computer will process the data that has been entered via the data input terminal. The central computer may deal with stock control and re-ordering of goods as necessary. You will also encounter data input terminals at your bank and in the travel agents when you go to book your holiday – the terminal can be used to display information and enter details of bookings.

Some data input terminals have limited processing capabilities, and these terminals are called *intelligent* terminals. Terminals with no processing capabilities are called *dumb* terminals.

1.4 Hardware

Hardware refers to any *physical* parts of your computer. The visual display unit (VDU) or monitor, printer, keyboard, mouse, trackerball, storage devices (hard drive, floppy disk), speakers, central processing unit, electronic components, boards, memory chips, etc. are all items of hardware.

Processing unit

The processing unit (either a desktop or tower metal or plastic box) contains these elements:

*   The *Central Processing Unit* (CPU) and other microchips.

*   A *hard disk drive* for storing programs and data.

*   A *floppy disk drive* which allows a floppy disk (sometimes called a diskette) to be used for storage.

*   A *CD-ROM drive* which can read information from a standard CD (similar to a music CD). The CD may contain music, software or data. Most applications are issued on CD.

♦ A *modem* which allows the PC to connect to the telephone system and use e-mail and the Internet (some PCs have an *external* modem rather than an *internal* one).

The CPU is often referred to as the *brain* of the computer. It performs the core processing, logic control and calculation work on the information which is either input by the operator or specified by the software. It controls the information flow between secondary memory and main memory. A CPU constructed on a single chip is called a *microprocessor*.

The *clock speed* of the CPU is the speed at which it can process information. It is measured in megahertz (MHz) or gigahertz (GHz). Mega = million, Giga = billion, Hertz = cycles per second. A clock speed of 600 MHz therefore means that the processor can operate at 600 million cycles per second. The clock speed is *one* of the factors that can influence a computer's performance. Generally speaking, the higher the clock speed the more expensive the computer. Intel (with its Pentium range) and AMD (with its K series) are the main producers and suppliers of microprocessors.

Input devices

An input device is any device that enables you to enter data or give instructions to your computer. The keyboard and mouse are the most commonly used input devices, but there are also others.

The **keyboard** is used to type information into your computer

A **mouse** allows data input by selecting options or by dragging and drawing on screen.

Trackerballs and **touchpads** are often found on laptops instead of a mouse. A trackerball is like an upside down mouse, and you use your fingertips to move the ball (which has the effect of moving the mouse pointer on the screen). A touchpad senses a fingertip being drawn across it and moves the mouse pointer on the screen accordingly.

Scanners are used to convert printed material into a digitized form that can be imported into an application package. The scanner will take a 'picture' of the printed material, which can then be stored or viewed on your PC. If you wish to scan in text and then manipulate it using a word processor, the scanner will need optical character recognition (OCR) software to convert the image into text.

A **graphics tablet** is a touch-sensitive pad with a stylus. The stylus can be used to write or draw freehand onto the pad, and the data is converted into a digitized form for the computer.

A **digital camera** can store photographic images in a digital format. The images can be downloaded from the camera into your PC, and edited, printed and stored.

With **voice recognition** a microphone is attached to a PC with appropriate voice recognition software. When you speak into the microphone, the speech will be converted into text, which can then be stored, edited and printed. This method of input could be very useful for visually or physically impaired PC users.

Joysticks are used to play games.

Output devices

An output device is one that allows what is on your PC to be seen or heard.

The **Visual Display Unit** (VDU) (or *monitor*) displays information that has been entered into the computer. Note this jargon:

◆ **Pixels** – dots of light on the screen.

◆ **Resolution** – the number of pixels on the screen. Generally speaking, the more pixels the better the picture. A resolution of 640 × 480 means that there are 640 pixels across, 480 down the screen. A resolution of 800 × 600 is also common.

◆ **Refresh rate** (or scan rate) – the frequency at which the screen image is redrawn; typically, 60 times per second.

The size of a VDU varies. The measurement quoted is for the *diagonal* measurement of the screen itself. Most PCs come with a 15" VDU as standard, with 17" monitors becoming standard on some systems (the more expensive ones). Prices are coming down and 17", 19" and 21" VDUs are becoming more affordable.

Speakers tend to come as standard on a *multimedia* PC, the type often purchased for home use. They may be self-powered, with a small amplifier built in, and usually require a soundcard to be fitted inside the computer.

Speech synthesizer software translates written text into audible speech. It has specialist uses, e.g. to help people with impaired vision or those with physical disabilities.

Printers

Printers are used to produce hard copy (a print out) of the data in your computer – text, graphs, pictures, etc. There are different types of printers, each with their own advantages and disadvantages. Inkjet printers are good for home use (or where low volume printing is required) – they are cheap, but the ink cartridges are quite expensive. Laser printers are good for business use. Though they are quite expensive to buy, the running costs are less when high volume is required. You may also come across a dot matrix printer – an older, noisier type of printer. Cheap, but not as popular as they once where.

Summary of printer types

♦ **Dot matrix** printers work using small pins which are grouped together to form letters. The pins hit a ribbon giving the letter shape. They are cheap to buy (usually less than £100) and to run, as ribbons last a long time. The output is reasonably quick, but of poor quality and they are relatively noisy. They are mainly used now to print invoices and other multi-part forms.

♦ **Inkjet** printers use a very fine spray of ink to form the letters and images. They cost from £50 to £250 ($80–$400), but replacement ink cartridges are expensive at £25 ($40) or more. Colour models give impressive results and are good for low-volume, home use. Speed 3–12 ppm (pages per minute).

♦ **Laser** printers use fine powder (toner) to create the pages. They are expensive to buy (£250–£3,000/$400–$5,000) but have low running costs per page. Quicker than other types at up to 24 ppm, they are a good investment for long-term, heavy use.

♦ **Plotters** are a specialized type of printer used in design environments for things like technical drawings or architectural plans. They can print out large, complex hard copies. The computer software controls a type of pen that moves in two dimensions over paper.

Peripherals

Any piece of equipment attached to a PC rather than built into it is called a *peripheral* device. Printers, scanners, external drives, speakers, etc. are all peripherals.

Input/output devices

Some devices can be used for *both* input and output, e.g. **touch screens**. They are *input* in that you can select options and give instructions by touching the appropriate bit of the screen and they are *output* in that they are screens, like VDUs that display data from your computer.

Storage devices

The unit of measurement used to describe storage capacity on computers are bits, bytes, kilobytes, megabytes and gigabytes. The capacity of disks and memory size are measured in these units. As storage capacity is constantly increasing, the measurements most often used are megabytes (Mb) and gigabytes (Gb).

Unit of measurement	
1 bit	The amount of storage space needed to hold either a 1 or 0 in memory.
1 byte	Is equal to 8 bits. Every letter or number is made up of 8 bits (one byte), so each letter or number takes up one byte of storage space.
1 kilobyte (Kb)	1024 bytes.
1 megabyte (Mb)	1024 Kb – about 1 million bytes. RAM memory (page 15) is usually quoted in Mb – typically a PC will have between 16 and 64 Mb of RAM (although more can be added if required). The standard high density floppy disks have a capacity of 1.44 Mb.
1 gigabyte (Gb)	1024 Mb – about 1 billion bytes. Hard disk sizes are usually quoted in Gb – on new PCs the hard disk is typically about 20 Gb.
1 trigabyte (Tb)	1024 Gb – about 1 trillion bytes.

Disks

Hard disks contain your application software and your data. PCs are sold with a hard disk drive (HDD) built in. You can buy additional HDDs to increase your storage space – you can get HDDs to fit inside your PC (an internal drive), or ones that plug into your PC but sit outside the unit as a *peripheral* (an external drive). External drives are more expensive than internal ones, and the cost of a drive increases with its capacity. The capacity of HDDs is constantly increasing but typically they store from 20 to 40 Gb.

The *access time* (the time taken for the unit to search for, identify and process data saved on the disk) of a HDD is measured in milliseconds (msec). In general, larger capacity HDDs tend to have a faster access time than smaller ones.

A **floppy disk** drive uses 3.5" disks. These store less information than HDDs, with a capacity of 1.44 Mb. The main other difference between HDDs and floppy disks is that the latter are removable. They are often used to take backup copies of data files, in case the original file becomes corrupted (damaged). Floppy disks are the cheapest type of storage media, but they are becoming less popular as higher capacity options become available at a reasonable price.

Disks can be bought pre-formatted or unformatted (you need to format disks before your computer can write to or read from them). See Chapter 2 for information on formatting disks.

Iomega **Zip drives** combine the portability of a floppy disk with a higher capacity disk (originally 100 Mb, with 250 Mb disks now on the market). The zip drives use special disks, which look similar to, but a little bigger than, floppy disks. Zip drives can be fitted internally or externally.

Compact disks (CD-ROM) have been used on PCs for several years. CD-ROMs are normally used for distibuting application packages, encyclopaedias, clip art, etc. as they can store up to 700 Mb of information. In addition to storage capacity, increased speed of access is another benefit of CDs.

CDs (like all other areas of IT) are continually developing. There are now CDs that you can write to, in the same way as a HDD. There are two types: CD-R (Recordable) and CD-RW (ReWriteable). With a CD-R you can record information once only – once you've recorded something on it you can't re-record. With a CD-RW you can record, and re-record, as often as you want – the disks are reusable.

DVDs (Digital Versatile Disks) are beginning to supersede CDs. They have storage capacities of 4–5 Gb. You can store audio, video or computer program data on a DVD. CD-ROMs can be used in a DVD drive, but a DVD disk will not operate in a CD drive. DVD-R (recordable) is also available.

The storage devices discussed above are sometimes referred to as *secondary storage*.

Types of memory

Random Access Memory (RAM) is often referred to as *main memory* or *primary memory*. The programs and data you are working on are stored in RAM. It is *volatile* – when the computer is switched off anything in RAM is lost. The CPU controls the flow of programs and data to and from RAM. Data that has been stored on disk is copied into RAM when you open the file to work on it.

PCs will typically have between 32 Mb and 128 Mb of RAM. Many new applications will not run satisfactorily on less than 32 Mb. It is possible to add more RAM if you wish.

Read Only Memory (ROM) is similar to RAM, but its contents are not lost when the computer is switched off. ROM is sometimes referred to as *secondary* memory. The CPU can read the contents of ROM, but can't add anything to it. ROM is also available on CDs and DVDs.

1.5 Software

Software refers to the programs that make your computer work. Software includes the operating system (essential to get your computer up and running) and the applications, e.g. software that lets you carry out specific tasks (word processing, spreadsheets, e-mail, databases, etc.).

Operating system

The OS is essential to the efficient running of the PC. It controls which operations are carried out and in what order they are done. It ensures that when you press a key, the instruction is translated into something the computer can work with.

When a computer is switched on it is said to *boot-up*. During the boot-up process it carries out a Power On Self Test (POST) to check that the hardware components and the CPU and memory are all present and functioning correctly. The next thing that the computer does when it boots-up is to locate and load the OS (or part of the OS). The OS is usually stored on disk, e.g in your Windows folder. The OS is loaded into RAM at this stage.

The OS that you will become familiar with when working through this book is Microsoft Windows – you may be using Windows 95, 98, 2000, Me, NT or XP. Each of these is a different version of Windows, with 95 being the oldest. As software develops and new or better features are added, a new version is released, identified by the version number. A new version of Windows is released approximately every two years. If you can use one version, you will quickly learn how to use any other.

Windows has a Graphical User Interface (GUI). It uses pictures (icons) to show the facilities available on the PC rather than words. You can select a feature by pointing to it with the mouse and then clicking on it to choose it. A GUI makes it much easier for a user to tell the system what to do. Apple Macs also have a GUI.

Application packages

Computer programs like word processing, spreadsheet, database, etc. are called application packages. These are separate from the OS, but they must be compatible with it. If you read the box of a package in a store, it will tell you what OS it is compatible with.

New versions of the main application packages are released about every two to three years. You may find yourself using Office 95, or 97, 2000 or XP. Each new version improves on the last (usually), or introduces something new, but the core functions and features have remained constant for many years.

Popular application software are:

- **Word processing** – used to produce reports, memos, letters, books – anything that is text based.

- **Spreadsheet** – where you can enter text and numbers, perform calculations on the numbers and produce graphs.

- **Database** – used to keep data on customers, suppliers, stock items, library books, etc. Data can be *extracted* using different criteria e.g. all the books in a library by a given author.

- **Presentation** – used to create sophisticated presentations with text, pictures, graphs, video and music.

- **Desktop Publishing** (DTP) – used for newsletters, posters, invitations, etc. where you want a lot of control over where text and graphics are placed on a page. The more sophisticated word processors have similar capabilities to a DTP package.

- **Graphic design** – allow designers to produce complex, detailed designs that can be edited quickly and easily.

- **Accounts** – used by companies to keep track of their cash flow.

- **Games** – loads are available, with something for every age group.

Many applications are sold as a *suite*, e.g. Microsoft Office or Microsoft Works. These contain a set of packages, e.g. word processing, spreadsheet, presentation, database, desktop publishing. Both Works and Office are popular suites found in the home and in businesses, though the applications in Office are much more powerful and sophisticated than those in Works.

1.6 PC performance

A number of factors can affect a computer's performance – the speed at which it operates. You can judge performance in a number of ways, e.g. the time it takes to open a file, or the time it takes to display a graphic. Things that may affect the performance are:

- The clock speed of the CPU
- The amount of RAM
- The size of the HDD
- The access speed of the HDD
- The access speed of any peripheral device that the computer gets information from e.g. modem, external drives.

For a PC to operate at its optimum level, the components must be balanced. There is little point having 128 Mb of RAM and a 30 Gb HDD on a computer with a 133 MHz chip – the slow processor speed would not get the best out of the memory or HDD.

The more applications that you run simultaneously, the more memory and processing power you require.

1.7 Information networks

Two or more computers connected together form a *network*. A network may consist of a couple of computers in the same office sharing a printer and files or thousands connected across the globe.

Local Area Network (LAN)

A LAN is made up of computers connected together by cables in the same building, or campus. PCs can be networked in a simple *peer-to-peer* setup that allows peripherals, e.g. printers, scanners to be shared. A user can also access files on another user's hard drive in this type of network.

Alternatively, PCs can be networked through a central computer (called a *server* or *file server*) where they can share drives and folders. Each user is allocated a specific area of hard drive on the file server for their own data files. The file server also stores main application software that can be run over the whole network e.g. e-mail, anti-virus, etc. Back-up procedures are simplified for the users as all files on the file server can be backed up at the same time (often at night, when most people have gone home) rather than each user having to back up the files from their own PC.

File servers are intended for business rather than personal use and they are more expensive than standard PCs.

Benefits of linking PCs together into a LAN are that several PCs can share the same peripherals, e.g. printer, scanner. The PCs can also share application and data files easily and they can communicate using e-mail (provided e-mail software is installed).

Wide Area Network (WAN)

Computers connected over a long distance are part of a WAN. Large organizations may use a WAN to connect their offices in different parts of the country. For example, an organization with branches in London, Cardiff, Leeds, Birmingham, Glasgow and Edinburgh may have the offices connected using a WAN (the computers at each branch would be connected using a LAN). The WAN could use leased lines (perhaps from BT or NTL) for the exclusive use of the organization.

The advantages of linking PCs to a WAN is that data can be transferred a long distance very quickly (e.g. from your London office to your office in Edinburgh).

A computer linked to another via a modem over the telephone line would be part of a WAN. Computers linked via the Internet form a WAN. A PC attached to a WAN can have access to huge amounts of information (on the Internet) and communicate with others using e-mail (which is much quicker than sending information using the traditional mail service).

Modem (modulator/demodulator)

This device is used to link computers to the telephone line. It converts (modulates) the digital signal from the computer into an analogue wave that can be transmitted across the telephone network, then changes the signal back from analogue to digital at the other end (demodulates). It is usually fitted internally.

Modems work at a variety of speeds or transfer rates (known as the *baud rate*) with 56,600 bps now being typical.

Integrated Services Digital Network (ISDN) and Public Switched Data Network (PSDN)

Instead of a dedicated link between one LAN and another i.e. a WAN, it is possible to dial-up digital connections when required. These connections are called *circuit-switched digital services*. The ISDN is an example of this type of system. The link is much faster than the PSDN – the analogue network that you are probably connected to when you use your telephone or PC from home. A digital network transfers data much quicker than an analogue one, there is no need for a modem, and the data transferred is much less susceptible to corruption (data getting lost, etc.).

Asymmetric Digital Subscriber Line (ADSL)

ADSL is a technology for transmitting digital information on existing phone lines to homes and businesses. Unlike the regular dial-up phone service, ADSL provides a continuously-available, 'always on' connection. ADSL simultaneously accommodates analogue (voice) information on the same line. Because the link is broadband (high-capacity), it can carry data much faster than a standard telephone line.

Internet

The Internet is a huge WAN, linking together computers from all over the world. To access the Internet you need:

- A computer linked to the telephone network via a modem (if you're linked to an analogue line) or a computer linked to the ISDN network using an ISDN adapter.

- Internet software, e.g. Internet Explorer.

- An account with an Internet Service Provider (ISP). Your ISP will provide you with a connection to the Internet – usually at the same rate as a local phone call.

You can access the World Wide Web via the Internet, send e-mails, access your company computer system, transfer files, etc.

Intranet

An intranet is essentially a private network that has Internet-like features, but it is restricted to operating on a company's internal network. Information is displayed on Web style pages, and hyperlinks allow you to jump from place to place, but you are only accessing your company data. An intranet has three attractive features often missing when it comes to Internet use – **speed**, **security** (it is a private internal network (LAN/WAN), protected from Internet users by a *firewall* (special security hardware and/or software)) and **control** (it is managed by your own staff).

Extranet

An extranet is a private network that uses the Internet technology and the public telecommunication system to securely share part of a business's information or operations with suppliers, customers, or other businesses. An extranet can be viewed as part of a company's intranet that is extended to users outside the company. Users can log into the extranet over the Internet by entering their username and password.

Virtual Private Network (VPN)

A VPN is a private data network that uses public telecommunications, including phone lines or the Internet, to create a 'tunnel' between a company's servers and remote users' PCs or laptops. They are increasingly popular with companies who have staff working at home or away from the office. VPNs enable enterprises to create global communication links quickly and economically.

WLAN (Wireless Local Area Network)

There has been a rise in wireless network computing in the past few years. Initially pretty much confined to university campuses, health-care, manufacturing and warehousing, it is now becoming more widely available to the general public. The number of *hotspots* in airport lounges, coffee shops, etc. is increasing. A **hotspot** is a location where high-speed Internet access is available to anyone with a Wi-Fi enabled computer, thanks to a Wireless Local Area Network (WLAN) access point. Many handheld and laptop computers are now *Wi-Fi* enabled. WiFi – a standard that allows your PC to access a WLAN, which in turn may allow access to the Internet and your e-mail. Many PDAs are fitted with this standard. Access coverage extends up to a 100m radius depending on location and equipment.

World Wide Web (WWW)

The WWW is a vast collection of information stored on *web pages* and on *web sites*. Anyone connected to the Internet can view, read, print and/or download the information held on the WWW using their Internet browser (usually Internet Explorer).

Search engines

The WWW contains a vast amount of information. To help users find information, a *search engine* can be used. There are several to choose from, including Google, AltaVista, Yahoo!, Excite. You can locate the search engines at their web sites e.g. **www.yahoo.com**. When using a search engine you enter the word or phrase you are looking for into a text field, and it then produces a list of web pages and sites that match your search words. Depending on how specific your request was, and on the search engine used, you may have a few sites suggested – or hundreds or thousands!

Electronic mail (e-mail)

If you have access to the Internet you can send e-mail to anyone else who is connected. An e-mail is a message that is sent over a LAN or WAN. You can send text, data, pictures, etc. Messages received can be read, replied to, forwarded to someone else, stored, printed or deleted as required. Everyone who uses e-mail has a unique address.

E-mail is very quick and cheap and compares very favourably with the traditional mail service.

1.8 Looking after yourself

A good workspace

It is important that the area you work in is comfortable and suitable to the type of work you are doing. If you are in an office, your working environment must conform to the relevant Health and Safety at Work (HASAW) legislation.

Things to consider when assessing whether or not the working environment is suitable for computer use include:

Lighting and ventilation, e.g.

- Provision of adequate lighting
- Positioning of VDUs – the screens should not flicker or suffer from interference, and they should be free from glare
- Provision of blinds if necessary to minimize the effect of direct sunlight on the VDU
- Provision of adequate ventilation

Operator comfort, e.g.

- Provision of movable keyboards
- Suitable desktop space
- There should be sufficient desk room and leg room to allow for posture changes
- Provision of a document holder at suitable height
- An adjustable chair
- Minimized printer noise (a particular problem with dot matrix printers)

Safety, e.g.

- No trailing cables or power leads
- No worn out or frayed power leads
- No overloaded power points
- No liquid near electrical components

Problems that may be experienced by IT workers include:

- Backache and pains in general associated with bad posture and sitting in the same position for too long
- Repetitive Strain Injury (RSI) – the result of poor ergonomics combined with repeat movements of the same joints over a long period of time
- Eye strain – caused by flickering VDUs and not taking regular breaks from the screen (10 minutes every hour is recommended)
- Back injuries due to lifting heavy objects, e.g. boxes of paper
- Electric shocks due to dangerous wiring or incorrect working practice
- Injuries resulting from tripping over trailing cables or other obstructions.

It is the employer's responsibility to ensure that appropriate provisions are made available to provide a safe and comfortable working environment, but the employees have a responsibility to make sure that they make use of them and go about their jobs in an appropriate manner.

1.9 Hardware and software security

Increased use and reliance on computers has resulted in a need for users to be aware of threats to the security of equipment and data and steps that can be taken to reduce the danger from these threats.

Your computer equipment and the data on it are very important resources. It is therefore important that you look after them and take precautions to ensure that, should anything happen, you can recover from the situation.

Hardware can be protected through insurance policies – if your PC is stolen or damaged you will be able to replace it. You can help minimize the risks to your hardware by ensuring that you lock your office/room and close the windows when you leave.

Your software will most probably have been installed from CD, and if it becomes corrupted you should be able to re-install it from your original disks (make sure these are kept in a safe place).

Protecting your *data* needs a bit more thought. Threats include:

◆ Power cuts (where any unsaved data will be lost);

◆ Serious hardware fault;

◆ Physical damage (perhaps as a result of flood or fire);

◆ Infection by a computer virus;

◆ Theft or other malicious act.

Lost files on a home computer may cause some inconvenience, but in a business losing data could ruin an organization.

To minimize the effect of such incidents, you should *back up* the data on your HDD regularly. You may just back up important files to diskette or to a zip drive, CD-R or CD-RW, or you may back up the whole drive.

In a business situation, backups may be done every few hours, at the end of each day, weekly, etc. – it depends on the organization and how much the files change in a period of time. Data is normally backed up overnight when most people aren't at work and the process is usually at least partially automated.

The media containing the backups is called the *backing store*. Ideally, this should be kept at a different location from the computer – at least in a different room, ideally in a different building.

All backup media should be kept in an environment that is safe against theft, flood and fire. A safe or vault is often used. Ideally more than one set of backup media should be kept.

The storage devices need to be large enough to hold all the files that are considered crucial to the operation of the organization. Specialized storage devices such as tape-streaming machines, or CD-R or multi-gigabyte HDDs may be used.

For a home PC user, floppy disks, a zip drive, CD-R or CD-RW can be used for backing up your data. Exactly how often you back up will vary from individual to individual – but if you've just spent hours working a project on your PC, it's a good idea to back up the files before you finish work.

Write protecting

To guard against floppy disks being accidentally overwritten, you can write-protect them. If you look at a disk, you will notice that the casing has two square holes through it. One of the holes has a sliding tab which you can move to open or close the hole. If this is open, the disk is write protected (you can open files from it, but you can't save to it).

Password protection

When working in a networked environment, password protection can help to ensure that only authorized users can access the system and open and edit the files held on it.

Password protection can be assigned at a *user* level (through the operating system) so that only authorized users can access the system. The computer pauses as it boots up and you must enter your user identification and password before you can go any further.

Some *folders* on the file server will be shared – several users may have access to them. To ensure that only authorized users access these folders, passwords may be assigned to them.

If you have *files* on the system that you don't want other users to be able to view or edit, you may be able to password protect the individual files (most modern applications allow the user to password protect individual files).

Different users can have different levels of security clearance assigned to them, allowing different users access to different parts of the system and its files.

Screen savers

Screen savers are used to prevent the VDU from becoming damaged by a static image displayed on it for a long period of time. If you use a screen saver on your PC, you can enter a password as one of the screen saver options. When the screen saver is displayed, it will be necessary for the password to be entered before the system can be accessed again.

Computer viruses

A computer virus is a piece of software that has been written often with the specific purpose of causing havoc on computer systems. It is called a virus because it has been programmed to spread through the system and on to other computer systems, just like an infectious virus spreads through the population. Some viruses are harmless, and do no serious damage, but serve to remind you just how vulnerable your system may be. Other viruses can have disastrous effects – deleting files, corrupting disks, etc.

No computer is immune to virus attack (although there aren't too many mainframe viruses), but some basic safety precautions can help limit the chances of infection:

- Install reliable anti-virus software on your computer, and update it regularly.

- Use the anti-virus software to scan your system regularly.

- Use the anti-virus software to scan any removable disks before you open files on them.

- Scan any files downloaded from the Internet before you open them – viruses can be transmitted in attachments to e-mails.

- Install only genuine software from reputable sources.

- Don't open e-mails from sources that you don't recognize.

- Don't open attachments to e-mails from sources that you don't recognize.

The virus writers are often a step ahead of the anti-virus software writers, so it is important to keep your anti-virus software up to date.

When you run your anti-virus software, it will disinfect any files that it finds with a virus it recognizes. If it cannot disinfect the file, it may 'quarantine' it, or delete it in an attempt to safeguard your machine.

1.10 Legal issues

There are some legal issues that computer users should be aware of.

Copyright

Software copyright legislation is in place to give the authors and developers of software the same rights as authors of published written or musical works.

When you buy software, you don't actually purchase the package, but you purchase a licence that allows you to use the software. Each licence that you purchase has an identification code – you can usually check the product ID in the product information screen (Help menu, About ….).

With some licences you are permitted to install a copy of the software on one computer, and take a backup copy of the software for security purposes. With other licences you may be able to install two copies of the software e.g. one on your office machine and one on your laptop or home PC. This option recognizes the fact that people often use the software in two locations, though they only use one copy at a time (you can't be in two places at once).

In a business situation, where you perhaps have 50 users on a network, you can buy a software licence that allows you to run the number of copies you require at any one time. This works out much cheaper than buying the same number of individual licences. The licence should cover the maximum number of users you expect to be using the software at any one time.

Copyright also applies to text, pictures, videos and music that you find on the Internet. If you download any of these items from the Internet with the intention of using them in your own work you should get permission from the copyright holder if at all possible. At the very least you should acknowledge your source.

Shareware

Shareware software is obtained on a kind of sale-or-return basis. You can obtain the software free, use it for a limited period e.g. 30 days, then, if you decide that you want to continue to use the software you should forward that appropriate fee (typically £10–£30) and become a registered user. At the end of the evaluation period the software may have been programmed to stop working or it may flash up messages telling you to pay up! Sometimes the evaluation copy of a shareware package will be a scaled-down version of the whole package. If you decide to pay up and register then the full package will be sent to you.

Freeware

Freeware is similar to shareware, but it doesn't cost anything. Freeware authors and developers often produce the software to solve a particular problem they have had, or just as a personal project/challenge. Once the software is written, they make it freely available to anyone else who thinks that they'll find it useful.

If you use shareware or freeware software try to ensure that it comes from a reputable source or is recommended in PC magazines, etc. The software may not have been tested as thoroughly as commercial software and it may contain bugs or viruses. There is however some very good, useful and safe shareware and freeware software available – just be careful!

Data Protection Act

The Data Protection Act appeared in 1984 in the UK, and it was updated in 1998. It states that users of personal data relating to living, identifiable individuals which is automatically processed should be registered with the Data Protection Registrar. The users of the personal data should then adhere to the Codes of Practice and Data Protection Principles set out within the Act. The rules that must be followed by all organizations keeping personal data on individuals are listed here.

The personal data must be:

* Obtained lawfully

* Held securely

* Used only for the purpose stated to the Data Protection Registrar (or compatible purposes)

- Adequate, relevant and not excessive in relation to the purpose for which it is held

- Accurate and kept up to date

- Deleted when it is no longer required

- Available to individuals so that they can access and check the information that is held on them

As most organizations hold personal data – on customers, employees, suppliers, patients, etc. – most organizations (even small ones) must be registered with the Data Protection Registrar.

1.11 Other terms you will meet

This section discusses some terms you may encounter as you read about developments in information technology.

Information Technology (IT) refers to any means of storing, processing and transmitting information using modern technology (computers). The term *Information and Communications Technology* (ICT) has also emerged. ICT encompasses facsimile, telephone, multi-media presentations, etc. as well as computers.

Information superhighway is used to describe a situation where information of any kind, anywhere in the world, is available to anyone who had access to a PC linked to the Internet. You can travel along the highway until you find what you are looking for.

The term *Information Society* may mean two things:

- A society where an increasing proportion of the working population are employed in collecting, processing, storing, retrieving and transferring information.

- A society where people have access to an almost unlimited amount of information via the Internet (in their homes or at work) without having to look it up in reference books or visit libraries.

E-commerce

The Internet has facilitated the expansion of e-commerce. Firms can advertise their products on their web sites on the Internet, take orders and accept payment via secure credit card transfer.

Many goods bought over the Internet are cheaper than they would be in the high street, as the company doesn't have the overhead of a shop front in a prime location. However, you have to decide what you want without actually seeing it (all you have is a picture on your screen), and this can be a disadvantage (unless you have already seen the product elsewhere).

There are obvious security issues with e-commerce. You must give your name and delivery address so that your purchases can be forwarded to you. You must also provide credit card information so that you can pay for the goods. Legitimate companies that conduct their transactions electronically take steps to ensure that their sites are secure and the information that you provide is safe.

As with all remote shopping, try to ensure that you do business with reputable companies. If a deal sounds too good to be true and the company is one that you haven't heard of, you would be wise to be wary.

Electronic Data Interchange (EDI)

This refers to a situation where all communications in a business transaction are done electronically. An example is computers in a retail environment. As items are purchased, details of the item are entered into the computer via the bar code reader at the checkout. This information automatically updates the stock records. When the stock levels reach the re-order level, an order would be raised and sent to the supplier electronically (using an EDI facility) and payment could be authorized at the same time. The supplier's computer would respond electronically to the order, arrange despatch of the goods and prepare and send the invoice.

Video conferencing

Business people world wide can have face-to-face meetings using video conferencing. Video cameras are linked via computers and the Internet so that people can see who they are talking to without leaving their office. A lot of time and money can be saved by holding meetings this way. People do not need to spend time and money travelling, or pay expensive hotel bills.

1.12 A changing world

The world of computers never stands still. From the time that I have written this book, until the time that you read it, there will be new developments and innovations.

To find out more, and keep up to date on what's going on, you can:

* Read articles on developments in ICT in the newspapers

* Read computer magazines

* Watch technology programs on the TV

* Surf the net

Summary

This chapter has introduced you to the world of ICT. It has discussed:

* The history of computers

* Computers in everyday life – at home, work and in education

* Different types of computer and the different parts of a computer

* Hardware and data security

* Software – operating system and application packages

* System development

* Information networks

* Health and safety issues

* Legal considerations

* Keeping up to date

02

windows
essentials

In this chapter you will learn

- how to start, stop and restart your computer
- about the desktop
- how to manage your files
- how to use the on-line help

2.1 Start, stop and re-start your PC

Switching on the computer

The exact location of the switches on a PC varies from model to model. Have a look at your PC and try to find the switches. The switch on the main unit (the box containing the hard drive, CPU, modem, etc.) will be somewhere on the front of the unit. The switch for the VDU (if it has one) will most probably be on the front of the unit, but it may be up the side or even on the back.

1 Ensure that your PC is plugged in and the power is switched on at the socket.

2 Press the ON/OFF button on the main unit.

3 Switch on the screen (if necessary – with some PCs the screen is switched on and off with the main unit).

4 Wait for a few seconds until the log-on screen appears. The one below is set up for four users.

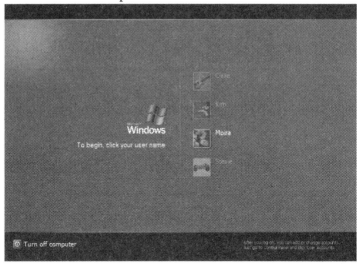

5 Click on your user name.

Your computer will display the *Desktop* (see section 2.2) ready for you to tell it what you want to do next.

If you switch on your computer and it doesn't work, do some basic checks before calling for help.

Check that:

* The cables are inserted into the back of the units properly.
* The computer is plugged in and switched on at the wall.
* The brightness control on the monitor hasn't been turned down.
* The screensaver hasn't just blanked the screen – move the mouse and wait a few seconds to see if your computer wakes up!

Log off or turn off the computer

* If you want to leave the computer on, ready for someone else to use, you should *log off.*
* If you have finished working on your computer altogether, you should *turn it off.*

To log off:

1 Close all your files and programs.
2 Click **Start** on the **Task Bar**.
3 Click **Log off**.
4 At the prompt, choose **Log off**.

* Windows will save your settings and return to the log-on screen.

To turn off your computer:

1 Click the **Start** button on the **Task Bar**.
2 Choose **Turn off computer**.
3 At the prompt, choose **Turn off**.

* If you are at the Log-On screen:

1 Click **Turn off your computer**.

There may be times when your computer 'hangs' and refuses to do anything. You may be able to restart it when this happens.

To restart the computer:

1 Click **Start**.
2 Choose **Turn off computer**.
3 Select **Restart**.

If this is not an option, press the Restart button (usually located on the front of your CPU). If all attempts to restart the computer fail, you will just have to switch it off (either at the on/off switch on the CPU, or at the wall if that fails) and try again!

2.2 The Desktop

The *Desktop* is the name given to the background area of the screen.

Icons – shortcuts to applications, folders or files

Start button opens the Start menu   Taskbar   Clock

Desktop icons can be moved. 'Drag and drop' them (click and hold down the left button, drag the icon to its new position and release the button), or get Windows to arrange the icons on the Desktop and position them automatically:

1 Right-click (click the right mouse button) anywhere on the Desktop.

2 A pop-up menu appears. Click (the left button) on the menu item **Arrange Icons By**.

3 Click **Name, Type, Size** or **Modified** as required.

or

◆ Click **Auto Arrange**.

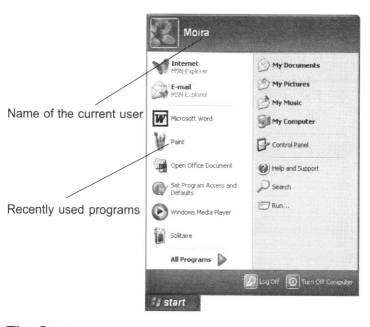

Name of the current user

Recently used programs

The Start menu

The Start menu is used to launch applications, get Help, etc.

To open it click ![start].

The Start menu gives a list of useful places on your PC e.g. My Documents, Control Panel and Help and Support, it also gives easy access to the Internet and e-mail, and your most frequently used programs (this is automatically updated as you use the PC).

The All Programs option will display a list of all the applications installed on your computer (not just the frequently used ones).

2.3 Working with windows

When you look at My Documents or at the Control Panel, the information is displayed in a window. When you open an application it will be displayed in a window.

It is important that you can recognize, name and know the purpose of the different parts of a window.

You should also know how to move and manipulate windows.

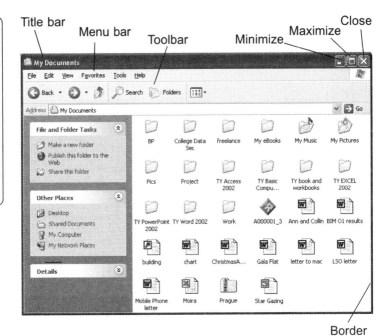

Title bar
Menu bar
Toolbar
Minimize
Maximize
Close

Border

Open *My Documents* so that you have a window to explore.

1   Open the **Start** menu (click **Start**).

2   Click **My Documents.**

Maximize/Restore Down

If a window is maximized it fills the whole screen – you cannot see any Desktop area behind it.

◆   To maximize a window click the **Maximize** button. It will then be replaced by the **Restore Down** button – click this to reduce the window to its size before it was maximized.

Minimize/restore

When you minimize a window, its name appears on the Taskbar and the window is tucked away so that you can see whatever is behind it – perhaps the Desktop, or another application window.

◆   Click the Minimize button to minimize a window.

◆   To restore a minimized window, click its name on the Taskbar.

Resize

If a window is not maximized you will be able to see its border. Drag its border to make the window larger or smaller. The mouse pointer becomes a double-headed arrow when it is over a border.

Move

Windows that are not maximized can be moved around the Desktop. Drag the title bar of a window to move it.

Close

◆ To close a window, click the Close button ▓ on its top right.

Have a look at some other windows and see if you can identify the different areas.

Some windows have scroll bars on them. You use the scroll bars to move up and down (or right and left) to display information that can't be fitted onto the screen.

You could also have a look at WordPad (open the **Start** menu, point to **All Programs**, then to **Accessories** and click on **WordPad**) or Paint (**Start > All Programs > Accessories > Paint**) and identify the different areas in the window.

Moving between open windows

If several windows are open you can move from one to another.

Either

◆ Click on the name of the window in the Taskbar.

Or

◆ Hold down [**Alt**] and press [**Tab**] repeatedly. You will cycle through the open windows. When the name of the one you require is displayed on the screen, release the keys.

Desktop shortcuts

If you use an application, folder or file regularly, you could create a *shortcut* to it from your Desktop so that you can access it quickly.

To create a shortcut on your Desktop:

1 Ensure that your Desktop is visible behind the Start menu or the My Documents window.

2 Locate the program in the **Start** menu, or the folder or file in *My Documents*, right-click on it and drag it onto the Desktop.

3 Release the mouse button.

4 A short menu will appear. Click **Create Shortcut(s) here**.

◆ The shortcut will appear on your Desktop as an icon.

Anytime that you want to access the application, folder or file, all you need to do is double-click the shortcut icon on the Desktop.

To remove a shortcut from your Desktop:

1 Select it (click on it).

2 Press [**Delete**].

This deletes the shortcut but not the application, folder or file.

2.4 The Menu bar

At the top of each window is the Menu bar. You can use this to access every command in that application. You can display the menus and select options using either the mouse or the keyboard.

Using the mouse:

1 Click on the menu name to display the options in that menu.

2 Click on the menu item you wish to use.

Using the keyboard:

1 Hold down [**Alt**].

2 Press the underlined letter in the menu name, e.g. [**Alt**]-[**F**] to open the File menu, [**Alt**]-[**V**] for the View menu.

3 Keep [**Alt**] held down and press the underlined letter in an option name to select it, e.g. O in the File menu to Open.

Or

◆ Use the up and down arrow keys on your keyboard until the item you want is selected, then press [**Enter**].

◆ Once a menu is displayed, you can press the right or left arrow keys to move from one menu to another.

To close a menu without selecting an item from the list:

◆ Click the menu name again, or anywhere off the menu list.

Or

◆ Press [**Esc**].

In addition to the menus, many of the features can be accessed using the toolbars or keyboard shortcuts.

2.5 The Control Panel

The Control Panel on your PC allows you to check and change the current system information and settings. Some of the information is hardware and software related (and you shouldn't change these unless you know what you are doing). Other settings allow you to customize your working environment – setting the time and date accurately, controlling the volume of your speakers, customizing your Taskbar, screensavers and Desktop settings. You should explore and experiment with these settings.

System information

Your computer will most likely consist of:

- A unit that contains the Central Processing Unit (CPU), RAM memory, modem, a hard disk (your C: drive), a CDRW or DVD drive (or a combined drive) and a 3½" diskette drive
- Keyboard
- Mouse
- Visual Display Unit (VDU)
- Printer
- Speakers.

There may be times when you need to know something about these devices. This is particularly the case when you intend to upgrade your software or hardware, or when speaking to someone about your hardware or software not performing well.

Do you know anything about the specification of your computer? If someone asked you how much RAM your computer had or what processor it used would you be able to tell them? You can easily find this information in the **System Information** dialog box.

To access System Information:

1 Open the **Start** menu.
2 Click **Control Panel**.
3 Select **Performance and Maintenance**.
4 At the **Pick a Task** list, choose *See basic information about your computer.*

The **System Properties** dialog box will appear.

The *General* tab contains basic system information about your PC.

The *Hardware* tab is used when you want to add new devices to your PC. You can also use it to display a list of the devices that are currently installed, and to change their properties or troubleshoot any problems.

In this example, you can see that the computer has the Microsoft Windows XP Home Edition operating system, a Celeron 2.2 GHz processor and 256 Mb of RAM.

Dialog boxes

A dialog box looks similar to a window, but has no minimize, maximize/restore down buttons – you can't change its size.

Dialog boxes are used to collect information or option choices from the users. They normally have an **OK** button, a **Cancel** button and sometimes an Apply button. If you change the information in a dialog box, click:

* **OK** to close the box and make the changes take effect
* **Apply** to apply the changes without closing the box
* **Cancel** to close the dialog box without any changes taking effect

Date & Time

At the far right of the Taskbar you will notice the clock. If you move your mouse pointer over it, the current date will appear.

To switch the clock display on or off:

1 Right-click on an empty area of the Task Bar.

2 Choose **Properties…** to display the **Taskbar** tab of the **Taskbar and Start Menu Properties** dialog box.

3 Select/deselect the *Show the clock* checkbox to switch the display on or off.

4 Click **OK**.

The date and time displayed on your clock should be accurate. If they are inaccurate, you can correct them:

1 Double-click on the time icon at the right of the Taskbar to open the **Date and Time Properties** dialog box. Make sure you are on the **Date & Time** tab.

To change the month:

2 Click the drop-down arrow beside the month field.

3 Select the month.

To change the year:

4 Click the split arrows to the right of the year field to change the year.

To set the date:

5 Select the date on the calendar.

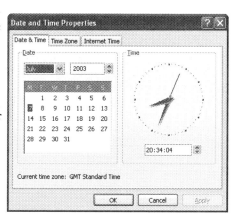

To set the time:

6 Double-click on the part of the time field that you wish to change – the hours, minutes or seconds.

7 Use the split arrows to the right of the field to increase or decrease the value as necessary, or type in the value required.

8 Click **Apply** or **OK**.

To change the time zone:

1 Click on the name at the top to open the **Time Zone** tab.

2 Choose the time zone required from the drop-down list.

3 Tick the ☑ Automatically adjust clock for daylight saving changes box to have your clock changed automatically each spring/autumn.

4 Click **OK**.

Volume settings

The volume settings used by your audio equipment may be controlled physically (by adjusting the volume on your hardware) or it may be possible to control the volume using software. You can adjust the volume of the warning sounds (e.g. the one you hear if you try to close a file without saving it) from the Control Panel.

1 Open the **Start** menu.

2 Click **Control Panel**.

3 Select **Sounds, Speech, and Audio Devices**.

4 Select a task from the list to adjust the system volume, sound scheme and speaker settings as required.

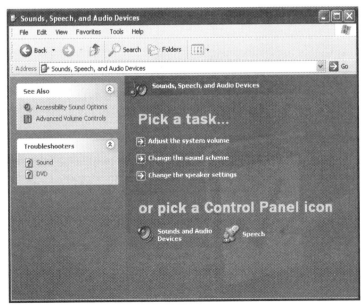

To toggle the display of the volume icon on the Taskbar:

5 Select **Sounds and Audio Devices**, then select the **Volume** tab.

6 Select/deselect the **Place volume icon in the Taskbar** option.

7 Click **OK**.

8 Close the **Sounds, Speech, and Audio Devices** window.

If the volume icon is displayed on your Taskbar, you can change the volume of audio devices from there:

1 Click the **Volume Control** button on the Taskbar.

2 Increase or decrease the volume as required.

3 Click anywhere on your screen to close the volume control.

Appearance and Themes

You can change the way that your Windows environment looks to suit your own preferences. The colour scheme, background, screen saver, user account picture, etc. can all be customized. When you log out, Windows will save your settings.

To access the Appearance and Themes options:

1 Open the **Start** menu.

2 Click **Control Panel**.

3 Select **Appearance and Themes**.

4 Pick a task from the list of options.

◆ The Display Properties dialog box will be displayed.

If you choose

◆ *Change the computer's theme*, the **Themes** tab is selected

◆ *Change the Desktop background*, the **Desktop** tab is selected

◆ *Choose a screen saver,* the **Screen Saver** tab is selected

◆ *Change the screen resolution,* the **Settings** tab is selected

To change the theme:

1 Select the **Themes** tab in the **Display Properties** dialog box.

2 Click the drop-down arrow to the right of the Theme list.

3 Select a theme.

4 Click **Apply** (if you want to keep the dialog box open) or **OK**.

The Themes tab of the Display Properties dialog box. A theme sets the background image, the colours and fonts used in windows, menus and dialog boxes, and the warning sounds. All these can be set individually – a theme gives you a matching selection.

To customize the Desktop:

1 Select the **Desktop** tab in the **Display Properties** dialog box.

2 Scroll through the list and select a background image.

3 Specify the display option – *Centre, Tile* or *Stretch.*

4 Click **Apply** (if you want to keep the dialog box open) or **OK.**

• If you select **None** in the background list, you can choose a colour for your Desktop from the color options.

To set a screen saver:

1 Open the **Screen Saver** tab in the **Display Properties** dialog box.

2 Click the drop-down arrow and select a saver from the list.

3 Click **Settings**, adjust the screen saver options as required and click **OK.**

4 Increase or decrease the **Wait time** as required (between 2 and 10 minutes is usually fine).

5 If you want to check your settings click **Preview.**

6 Click **Apply** or **OK.**

To change your user account picture:

1 Click **User Account Picture** in the *See Also* list on the top left of the **Appearance and Themes** window.

2 Scroll through the pictures and select the one required.

3 Click **Change Picture**.

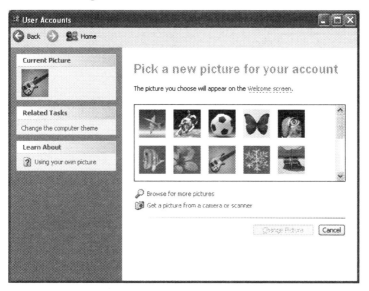

2.6 Formatting floppy disks

Most of the time you will probably save your work to the hard drive (C:) or to a network drive (H, J, Y, etc.). There may be times however when you need to use a floppy disk, e.g.

- in a school or college situation where you do not have storage space allocated to you on the hard drive or network drive

- to move information from one PC to another

- to take a copy of some data files for security purposes.

If you are going to use floppy disks, they must be formatted before you can store information on them. You can buy boxes of disks that are pre-formatted, but some are sold unformatted.

You can also format disks that have already been used. Those that have been around for some time and have had a lot of use will benefit from a re-format. When you format disks that contain data the data is erased (so be careful that you don't format one that contains something that you want to keep).

To format a floppy disk:

1 Insert the disk into the (A:) drive (the metal part goes in first, label facing upwards).

2 Click **Start**, then **My Computer**.

3 Right-click on the *3½ Floppy (A:)* icon.

4 A short menu will appear. Click on **Format...**

5 Specify any options as required.

6 Give your diskette a label (name) if you wish.

♦ If you need information on any of the options, click the question mark at the top right of the **Format** dialog box, then click on the option – a brief explanation of the option will be displayed

7 Click **Start**.

8 Click **OK** at the warning about all data being erased.

9 Wait while your diskette is formatted.

10 Click **OK** when the format is complete.

2.7 Help and Support Center

The Help and Support Center is a central point from which you can get access to a huge amount of information to support you as you work.

To access the Help and Support Center:

1 Open the **Start** menu.

2 Choose Help and Support . The Home page of the Help and Support Center will be displayed.

You can interrogate the Help system in a variety of ways.

To browse the Help system:

♦ Click the topic that you are interested in on the Home page.

Have a look at Windows Basics – it has lots of useful information!

Type a word you want Help on

Start searching

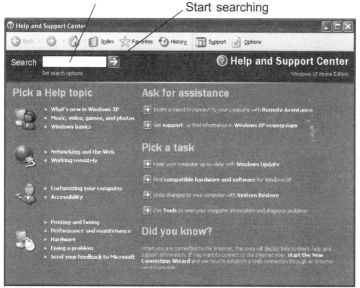

To search for Help:

1 Type the word(s) that you want Help on into the **Search** field.

2 Click the Start Searching button, or press [**Enter**].

To use the Index:

1 Click 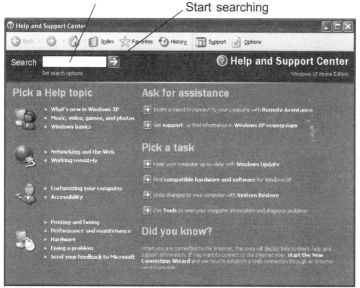 I̱ndex on the toolbar.

2 Type in the keyword(s) to find, e.g. "new folder".

3 Press [**Enter**].

To return to a page that you've already visited:

◆ Click Back until you reach the page

Or

1 Click History to display the list of pages already visited.

2 Select the page required.

3 Click **Display**.

◆ Once you've used Back to return to a page, you can use
to go forward through the pages visited again.

Favorites

If you find a Help page that you know you will want to revisit regularly, you could add it to your Favorites.

To add to Favorites:

1 Display the Help page required.

2 Click 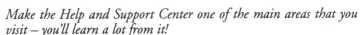 Add to Favorites .

To go to a Favorite page:

1 Click ⭐ Favorites .

2 Select the page that you wish to go to.

3 Click **Display**.

* You can return to the Home page at any time by clicking 🏠 on the toolbar.

Make the Help and Support Center one of the main areas that you visit – you'll learn a lot from it!

2.8 File management

The programs and data that are stored on your PC are stored on disks which are housed in drives. The drives are named using letters of the alphabet. Your diskettes use the A: drive. Your local hard drive is the C: drive. Your CD-ROM drive is probably your D: drive. You may have other drives, e.g. zip drives for backups, or there may be network drives available to you. They will be named E:, F:, G:, H:, etc.

We have already seen that you can display the contents of your computer system and disks in *My Computer*, and the contents of your own work area using *My Documents*.

As you increase the use that you make of your computer, you will eventually end up with lots of files in *My Documents*. It is important that you organize them, so that you can find any file easily.

You can organize your files in much the same way as you would a manual filing system – by setting up folders for your work and storing your documents within the folders.

Folders and files

Imagine you are secretary of a local Wine Appreciation Society, and you've decided to create a new folder within *My Documents* for the files that you create for this important institution.

To make a new folder:

1 Display *My Documents*, or open the folder (double-click on it) that you wish to make a new folder within.

2 Click ![Make a new folder].

3 Type in the folder name.

4 Press [Enter].

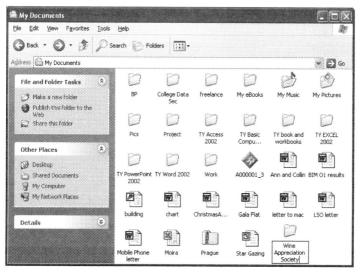

To display your folders/files using a different view:

1 Click the drop-down arrow by the **View** tool.

2 Select a view.

Details view gives information on the size, type and date that the file was modified. You can sort the files into order on any column by clicking on the heading of the column.

File types

Different file types are created by different applications. You can identify the files types from the icons beside the file names, e.g.

Star Gazing	letter to mac	Moira	building	1b
PowerPoint	Word	Excel	Access	Bitmap

or by the three-character extension at the end of the file name (if it is displayed).

You can toggle the display of the extensions:

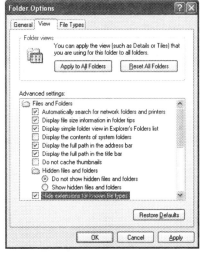

1 From the **Tools** menu in *My Documents*, choose **Folder Option…**

2 Select the **View** tab.

3 Scroll through the options until you find the *Hide extensions for known file types* checkbox.

4 Select or deselect the checkbox as required.

5 Click **OK**.

You should be familiar with these common file extensions.

Extension	Application	File type
mdb	Access	Database
doc	Word	Word processing
xls	Excel	Spreadsheet
bmp	Paint	Bitmap image file
pub	Publisher	Desktop publishing
ppt	PowerPoint	Presentation graphics
htm/html	various	Web page
rtf	various	Word processing

You can easily rename any folder or file if you consider the current name unsuitable.

To rename a folder or file:

1 Select the folder or file.

2 Click  (or **Rename this file**).

3 Type in the new name for the folder or file.

4 Press [**Enter**].

To move a folder or file:

1 Select the folder or file.

2 Click (or **Move this file**).

3 Indicate where the folder or file is to be moved to.

4 Click **Move**.

To copy a folder or file:

1 Select the folder or file.

2 Click (or **Copy this file**).

3 Indicate where the folder or file is to be moved to.

4 Click **Copy**.

Backups

A very important way of trying to ensure the security of your data is to back it up. This means that you take a copy of any important data – anything that you can't afford to lose.

Companies often have automated backup procedures where their data is backed up every few hours, or overnight. If you are working at home, or in a small business, it will probably be up to **you** to remember to back up your data.

You should regularly copy any important data files to a removable storage device, e.g. a floppy disk, zip disk or CD. On a home computer, the usual backup device is now a CD-RW. It is cheap, and stores 650 or 700 Mb of data.

Deleting a folder or file

This is a two-step process. When you delete a folder or file it is placed in the Recycle Bin. If you then realize that you should not have deleted it, you can restore it from there.

You can empty the Recycle Bin at any time.

1 Select the folder or file.

2 Click ✕ Delete this folder (or **Delete this file**).

Or

♦ Press [**Delete**].

3 Confirm the deletion at the prompt – click **Yes** to delete, or **No** if you've changed your mind.

Recycle Bin

To open the Recycle Bin:

♦ Double-click the Recycle Bin icon on the Desktop

To restore a folder/file that has been placed in the Recycle Bin

1 Select the folder or file(s).

2 Click Restore this item.

The item will be removed from the Recycle Bin and returned to the folder it was deleted from.

To restore all items that are in the Recycle Bin:

♦ Click Restore all items.

To empty the Recycle Bin:

♦ Click Empty the Recycle Bin.

Compression

Some files, particularly those that contain graphics and lots of formatting, can become quite large. If you have plenty of room on your disk this poses no problem, but if you are short of disk space you could *compress* the file to make it smaller.

If you want to send a large file to someone – either by e-mail or by copying it onto a floppy disk – you might need to compress it to make it smaller.

To compress a file:

1 Open *My Documents* (or the folder that contains the file).

2 Right-click on the file and choose **Properties**.

• Note the *Size* and *Size on disk* fields – they will be fairly similar.

3 Click *Advanced* in the **Attributes** options.

4 Select the *Compress contents to save disk space* checkbox.

5 Click **OK** to return to the **Properties** dialog box, then click **OK** to close it.

• Display the **Properties** dialog box again. You should see that the *Size on disk* field is smaller than the *Size* field.

• Repeat the steps, clearing the box at step **4**, to uncompress a file.

Searching for folders or files

If you have forgotten where a file is stored, you can *search* for it.

1 Open the **Start** menu and click 🔍 Search .

Or

2 Click 🔍 Search on the toolbar in *My Computer*.

• The **Search Results** window is displayed

3 Choose what you want to search for, e.g. **Documents**.

You can search on several different criteria or a mixture of criteria.

4 Enter all or part of the document name.

5 If you know a key word or phrase that occurs in the document, enter it into the appropriate field.

6 Tell the search which drive or folder you want to look in.

In addition you can…

7 Specify the date criterion.

8 Give an indication of document size.

9 To be more specific, click *More advanced options*, then:

• Choose whether or not to search subfolders.

• Indicate whether or not the file name is case-sensitive.

10 Click **Search**.

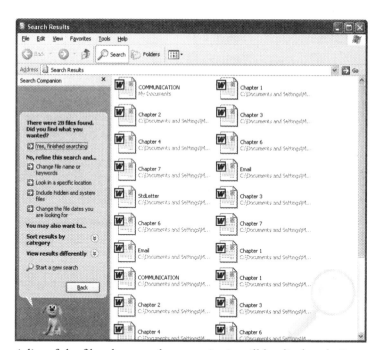

A list of the files that match your criteria will be displayed. Once you've found the file, double-click on it to open it.

Searching for specific file types

If you want to display all the Word files, or all the Excel files, you can do so easily as long as you know your file extensions (see page 50). Type the extension in the *All or part of the document name* field, e.g. '.doc'. When the search is complete, the files of the type specified will be displayed, together with the total number found.

Read only files

If you have files on your computer that you don't want changed, you can make them *read only*. They can be opened but not edited.

To make a file read only:

1 Display *My Documents*.

2 Right-click on the file you want to make read only.

3 Choose **Properties**.

4 On the **General** tab select the **Read-only** checkbox.

To make a file read/write again, simply deselect the Read-only checkbox on the General tab.

2.9 Printers

Windows has 'plug-and-play' technology which allows it to recognize many printers and install them automatically. It doesn't always work, so you should know how to install a printer yourself.

To install a printer:

1 Connect the printer to your computer following the manufacturer's instructions.

2 Open the **Control Panel**.

3 Choose **Printers and Other Hardware**.

4 Click **Add a Printer**.

5 Follow the instructions on the screen.

Default printer

Your computer system may be set up so that you can print your files to one of several different printers – a laser, an inkjet, etc. When you print a file from an application it uses the *default* printer – the printer that's been set up as the one that you normally print to. You can change the default printer. The printer that you want to become the default must be installed before you do this.

1 Open the **Control Panel**.

2 Choose **Printers and Other Hardware**.

3 Click **Printers and Faxes**.

4 Right-click on the printer that you wish to become the default printer.

5 Select **Set as Default Printer**.

The default printer will have a tick beside it.

The print queue

If you have sent several files to print, you may want to check on their progress. You can display the files that are in the print queue.

1 Open the **Control Panel**.

2 Choose **Printers and Other Hardware**.

3 Click **Printers and Faxes**.

4 Double-click on a printer to display the print queue.

You can use the menus in the print queue window to pause printing, purge print jobs (empty the queue), etc.

* To pause or resume printing of an individual document, right-click on it and select the option from the menu.

* To pause or resume printing of all documents sent to a printer, right-click on the printer and select the option from the menu.

Print screen

If you want to take a printout of exactly what is on the screen of your computer:

1 Press **[Print Screen]** (usually to the right of the Function keys on your keyboard).

2 Go to a document (in WordPad or Word) or run Paint.

3 Open the **Edit** menu and click **Paste**.

4 The document can be printed in the normal way, or from Paint you can save the screenshot as an image.

2.10 Installing software

Even if Windows XP and standard application software, e.g. Works or Office, were preinstalled on your computer when you bought it, you will most likely want to install some new software at some stage – perhaps a game or desktop publishing software.

Nearly all new software is supplied on a CD, and installing it is usually an easy procedure.

1 Insert the CD into your CD drive.

2 Follow the instructions on the screen.

If the CD does not start the setup process automatically, check the package for instructions.

You will probably be instructed to do this:

1 Open the **Start** menu and choose **Run…**

2 Type **D:setup.exe** into the **Open...** field (where D: is your CD drive).

3 Follow the instructions on the screen.

Or

1 Open the **Start** menu and choose **Control Panel**.

2 Select **Add and Remove programs**.

3 Click **Add New Programs**.

4 Choose **CD** or **Floppy**.

5 Follow the instructions on the screen.

Ensure that you purchase your software from a reputable supplier. Pirate software is illegal, and may be a source of computer viruses.

Summary

This chapter has introduced you to essential basic Windows skills. You have found out about:

- Starting, stopping and re-starting your computer
- The Desktop and working with windows
- Menus
- The Control Panel – system information, date & time, volume settings, themes, screen savers, etc.
- Formatting diskettes
- Online Help
- Creating and managing folders
- Copying, moving and deleting folders and files
- Backups
- File compression
- Printers – installing, setting the default printer and checking progress of print jobs
- Print Screen
- Installing software

03 common skills

In this chapter you will learn

- standard filing and printing techniques
- about the on-line Help
- how to format, search and spell check text
- about drawings and pictures
- how to manage toolbars

3.1 Open and close applications

1   Click the applications icon on the Desktop, if present.

Or

2   Click the **Start** button on the Taskbar.

3   Choose **All Programs**.

4   Click the application if you can see it in the list, e.g. Excel.

Or

5   Point to a program group to open its submenu and select the application from there, e.g. **Accessories** then **WordPad**.

Closing an application

♦   Click the **Close** button ✖ at the right of the application Title bar.

3.2 MS Office Help

As you work with your applications you will most probably find that you come a bit unstuck from time to time and need Help! There are several ways of getting Help – most of them very intuitive and user friendly. The Help system works in the same way in all Office applications.

Office Assistant

To call on the Office Assistant:

♦   Press [**F1**] or click the application **Help**
    ⑦ tool on the Standard toolbar.

Depending on what you have been doing, the Assistant may display a list of topics that you might be interested in.

To choose a topic from the 'What would you like to do?' list, simply click on the topic.

If you have a specific question, type it in at the prompt and click the **Search** button.

The Assistant will display the Help page.

Some Help pages contain text in a different colour.

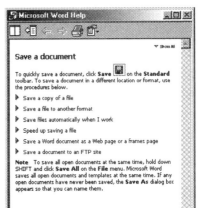

* If the text is part of a list it will expand to display more information.

* If the coloured text is embedded within the main text it is probably a phrase or some jargon that has an explanation or definition attached to it.

* Simply click the coloured text to display or hide the additional information.

When you've finished exploring the Help system, click the Close button at the top right of the Help window.

The Office Assistant can remain visible as you work on your file, or you can hide it and call on it as required. You can drag and drop it to reposition it on the screen.

* If you leave the Office Assistant displayed, click on it any time you want to ask a question.

* To hide the Office Assistant, right-click on it and choose **Hide** from the pop-up menu.

* To show it again, press **[F1]** or open the **Help** menu and select **Show the Office Assistant**.

* To change the way the Office assistant works, right-click on it and choose **Options** from the pop-up menu. Set the options required in the **Office Assistant** dialog box.

Tips

The Office Assistant is constantly monitoring your actions. If it thinks that it has a tip that may be useful to you, a light bulb will light up beside it. To read its tip, click the bulb.

Ask a Question box

You can also access the Help system using the **Ask a question box** on the Menu bar. Type in your question and press [**Enter**]. Choose the Help topic required from the list that is displayed – click on it!

[Ask a Question box screenshot showing "how do I underline" with options: Add a line; About symbols and special characters; Add a border; Underline text; Show or hide wavy underlines; See more...]

What's This?

If you haven't used Microsoft Office products before, or if you're new to Windows, there will be many tools, menus, buttons and areas on your screen that puzzle you. The **What's This?** feature can help you here – it works best when a file is open, as most of the tools, menus and screen areas are then active.

1 Hold down [**Shift**] and press [**F1**].

2 Click the tool.

Or

3 Open the menu list and click on the option.

Or

4 Click on the item or screen area.

If you accidentally invoke **What's This**, press [**Esc**] to cancel it.

Contents, Answer Wizard and Index

Whether or not you opt to use the Office Assistant, the **Help** tool or the **Help** menu option 🔃 will open the on-line Help system.

You can interrogate the Help system using the **Contents, Answer Wizard** or **Index** tabs. Click the 🔃 tool in the Help window to toggle the display of the tabs.

Contents tab

You can browse through the Help system from the **Contents** tab.

◆ Click the [+] to the left of a book to display or the [–] to hide its list of contents.

When a book is open, you will be presented with a list of topics.

To display a topic:

1   Click on it.

2   Browse the Help system until you find the Help you need.

To print a topic:

•   Click the **Print** tool 🖨 in the Help window when the topic is displayed.

To revisit pages you've already been to:

•   Click **Back** ⬅ or **Forward** ➡ to move through the pages.

To tile the Help window with your document window:

•   To be able to read the Help page while working on your file, click the **Auto Tile** tool ⊞ to arrange the Help and document windows side by side on screen.

Answer Wizard

If you want to interrogate the Help system by asking a question, try the **Answer Wizard** tab.

1   Enter your question, e.g. 'How do I create a table' and click **Search**.

2   Select a topic from the **Select topic to display** list.

•   The Help page will be displayed.

Index tab

If you know what you are looking for, the **Index** tab gives you quick access to any topic and is particularly useful once you are familiar with the terminology used in your application.

1   At the **Help** window, select the **Index** tab.

2   Type in the word you're looking for in the **Type keywords** field and click **Search**.

Or

3   Double-click on a word in the **Or choose keywords** list.

4   Choose a topic from the **Choose a topic** list.

5   Work through the system until you find the Help you need.

•   Close the Help window when you've finished.

ScreenTips

If you point to any tool on a toolbar, a ScreenTip will probably appear to describe its purpose. If no ScreenTips appear, you can switch them on if you want to.

1 Point to any toolbar that is displayed and right-click on it.

2 Choose **Customize...** from the shortcut menu.

3 In the **Customize** dialog box select the **Options** tab.

4 To switch the ScreenTips on, select the **Show ScreenTips on toolbars** option (or deselect it to switch them off).

5 Click **Close**.

Dialog Box Help

When you access a dialog box, e.g. the **Customize** one above, you can get Help on any item within it that you don't understand.

To get Help in a dialog box:

1 Click the Help button at the right of the title bar.

2 Click on the option, button or item.

♦ A brief explanation of the item will be displayed.

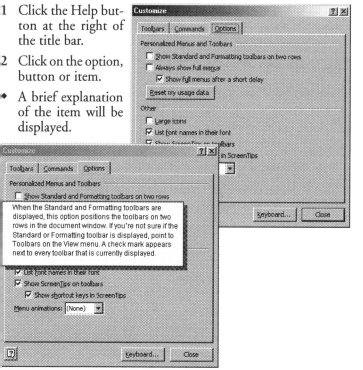

3 Click anywhere within the dialog box to close the explanation.

The Help tool that appears at the bottom left of some dialog boxes gives another route into the Help system.

Help on the Web

If you can't find the Help that you need in the standard Help system, you can always look on the Web.

* When you click the Office Assistant you will find an option to get Help from the Web at the bottom of the list of topics.

* In the Help menu, you will find an **Office on the Web** option.

The Help system is a valuable resource – don't be afraid to access it and explore. Dip in and out of it in whatever application you are using – it doesn't take too long to get used to it.

3.3 File handling

File handling routines that are similar across applications include creating a new file, opening, printing, saving and closing files.

The Task Pane

When you open an application, the Task Pane for creating and opening files is usually displayed on the right of the window, and a new file is created. To work on the new file, close the Task Pane (click the Close button at its top right) to give you more room for your file. You can open an existing file from the Task Pane – choose it from the list of file names or click the **More...** option.

If you don't want the Task Pane when you start an application, deselect the **Show at startup** checkbox at the bottom of the pane.

You can display the Task Pane at any time using the **View** menu:

1 Open the **View** menu.

2 Select **Task Pane**.

Create a new file

To create a new file using the default layout in any application

* Click the **New** tool 🗋 on the Standard toolbar.

A new file will appear, e.g. *Document2, Book2*, (the number in the file name depends on how many files you have created in this working session).

Open an existing file

If you want to view, update or print a file that you have saved and closed you must open the file that you want to work with.

1 Click the **Open** tool [image] on the Standard toolbar.

• The **Open** dialog box will appear on your screen.

2 Locate the drive and/or folder in which the file is stored.

3 Select the file you wish to open – click on its name.

4 Click **Open**.

• You can also open a file by double-clicking on its name in the **Open** dialog box.

If the file you want is a recently used one you will find its name at the bottom of the File menu. You can open your file from here, rather than go through the Open dialog box.

1 Open the **File** menu.

2 Click on the file name you want to open.

File	
Open...	Ctrl+O
Save As...	
Page Setup...	
Print...	Ctrl+P
1 C:\My Documents\...\Chapter 8.doc	
2 C:\My Documents\...\Chapter 5.doc	
3 C:\My Documents\...\Chapter 6.doc	
4 C:\My Documents\...\Chapter 4.doc	

If you wish to open more than one file simultaneously, select the files in the **Open** dialog box, and then click **Open**.

To select a group of adjacent files:

1 Click on the first file or folder.

2 Hold down [**Shift**].

3 Click on the last file or folder.

To select several non-adjacent files:

1 Click on the first file or folder.

2 Hold down [**Ctrl**].

3 Click on each of the other files or folders as required.

Moving between open files

If you have more than one file and/or application open, you will
see their names displayed on the Taskbar at the bottom of your
screen. If you point to the Taskbar button, the full name of the file
or application will be displayed. To move from one file to another,
click on the Taskbar button of the one that you want to display.

* You can also use the **Window** menu to go from one open file
  to another within the same application – you will find a list of
  your open documents at the end of it. Just click on the document you want to display.

Save and Save As

If you want to keep your file, you must save it. If you don't save
your file it will be lost when you exit your application. You can
save your file at any time – you don't have to wait until you've
entered all your text or data and corrected all the errors.

1 Click the **Save** tool 💾 on the Standard toolbar.

2 At the **Save As** dialog box select the folder you want to save
   your file into (the default is the Desktop in WordPad, My Documents in Office applications).

3 Give your file a name.

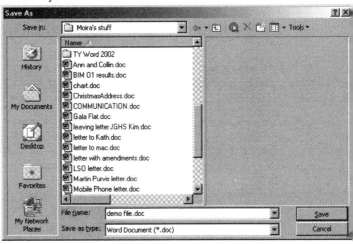

4 Leave the **Save as type:** at the default e.g. Word Document in Word, Microsoft Excel Workbook in Excel.

5 Click **Save**.

♦ The name of your file will appear on the Title bar in place of the temporary file name.

As your document develops, you can re-save your file any time you wish – just click the Save tool 🔲 again. The **Save As** dialog box will not open, but the old version of the file on your disk will be replaced by the new, up-to-date version displayed on your screen.

There may be times that you save a file, edit it, then decide that you want to save the edited file but also keep the original version of the file on disk. If you don't want to overwrite the old file with the new version, you should save it using a different file name, or to a different drive and/or folder.

1 Open the **File** menu and choose **Save As**.

2 The **Save As** dialog box will appear again.

3 Change the drive or folder if you wish.

Or

4 Enter a new name in the **File name** field.

5 Click **Save**.

File formats for other applications

If the file you have created is going to be opened in a different application, it may be necessary to save it in a different file format. For example, if you have created a file in Word XP and you are going to send the text to someone who wants to open the file in WordPerfect, you should save the file as a WordPerfect file, or a Text file, so that they can open it successfully. In some file formats some (or all) of the formatting may be lost.

To save in a different file format:

1 Click the **Save** tool or choose **Save As** from the **File** menu.

2 Select the drive and/or folder and name the file as usual.

3 Select the appropriate file format from the **Save as type** list.

4 Click **Save**.

3.4 Print and Print Preview

It is usually best to preview a file before you print it, so that you can check that it looks right before you waste paper and cartridges printing something that you later decide is unusable.

Print Preview

To preview a file:

• Click the **Print Preview** tool 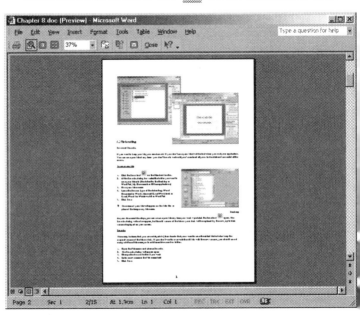 on the Standard toolbar.

The preview screens of applications vary a bit, but you can usually move between the pages in your file, zoom in and out, change the page setup, e.g. margins, orientation, and print. We will look at areas specific to each application in the appropriate chapter.

Print

To print one copy of a file on the default printer, click ▨ the **Print** tool on the Standard toolbar. In some situations, particularly in an office environment, there may be several printers on the network that you can print to. Only one printer can be the default, but you can easily print to any other installed printer.

1 Open the **File** menu and choose **Print**.
2 Select the printer required in the **Name** field.
3 Set other options as required.
4 Click **OK**.

If you don't have a printer attached to your computer, or if you want to print out your file on a printer that doesn't have the application that you are using on it, you can print to a file. The file can then be printed out on any PC.

To print to file:

1 Open the **File** menu and choose **Print**.
2 In the Name field select the printer that will be used to print out the file.
3 Select the **Print to file** check box.
4 Click **OK**.
5 In the **Print to file** dialog box select the drive and or folder if necessary and give your file a name.
6 Click **OK**.
◆ Once you've finished working on your file you should close it.

Closing files

◆ Open the **File** menu and choose **Close**.

Or

◆ Click the Close button ![close] at the top right of the file Title bar.

You will be prompted to save the file if it has changed since the last time you saved it.

Smart tags

As you work with your applications you will notice that 'smart tags' appear at various times, e.g. when Word automatically changes something, such as capitalization, when you paste an item, when using automatic numbering, etc. If you click the smart tag it will display a list of options that allow you to control or customize the task that you are performing.

3.5 Delete, Cut, Copy and Paste

Delete

If you have a large piece of text or data to delete, it will usually be quicker to select it and then press [**Delete**] or [**←**] (Backspace), rather than press the keys repeatedly.

To delete a chunk of text or data:

1 Select it.

2 Press [**Delete**].

Cut, Copy and Paste

There will be times when you have entered the right information into a file but it is in the wrong place. When this happens you should move or copy the object, e.g. text in Word, data in cells in Excel, or a picture in any application, to the correct location.

♦ If you want to remove an object from its current position, and place it somewhere else within your file you can *move* it.

♦ If you want to keep the object, but repeat it in another place in your file (or in another file), you can *copy* it.

You can move or copy an object within or between files. Before you can move or copy something you must select it.

To move or copy text or data

1 Select the object that you want to move.

2 Click the **Cut** tool [image] to move or the **Copy** tool [image] to copy (they're on the Standard toolbar).

3 Position the insertion point where you want the object to re-appear.

4 Click the **Paste** tool [image] on the Standard toolbar.

The object will appear at the insertion point.

♦ To specify the format of the pasted item, click the **Paste Options** smart tag (it appears below your pasted item) and select the option required.

Office Clipboard

If you cut or copy a couple of items, the Office Clipboard Task Pane will appear automatically. You can also display it by choosing Office Clipboard from the Edit menu. The Task Pane displays a list of the cut or copied items.

You can store up to 24 items in the Office Clipboard.

To paste an individual item from the Clipboard, click on it.

To paste all items, click **Paste All** at the top of the pane.

To empty the Clipboard, click **Clear All**.

To specify how you want the Office Clipboard Task Pane to work, click **Options** and set the options as required.

A Clipboard icon appears on the Taskbar when the Task Pane is displayed.

Click the Close button at the top right when you have done.

Cut or Copy to a different file

To move or copy an object from one file to another:

1 Open the file you want to move or copy the object from (the source).

2 Open the file you want to move or copy it to (the destination).

3 Display the source file.

4 Select the object to move or copy.

5 Click the **Cut** or **Copy** tool on the Standard toolbar.

6 Display the destination file.

7 Position the insertion point where you want the object to go.

8 Click the **Paste** tool on the Standard toolbar.

Drag and drop

As an alternative to using Cut or Copy and Paste to move and copy objects, try *drag and drop*. This is especially useful when moving or copying an object a short distance – i.e. to elsewhere on the screen. If you try to drag and drop over a longer distance, you will probably find that your file scrolls very quickly on the screen and that it is very difficult to control.

To move:

1 Select the object that you want to move or copy.

2 Position the mouse pointer anywhere over the selected object.

3 Click and hold down the left mouse button (notice the 'ghost' insertion point that appears within the selected area).

4 Drag the object and drop it into its new position.

To copy with drag and drop, hold down [**Ctrl**] while you drag the object.

Undo, Redo

To Undo an action:

♦ Click the **Undo** tool [icon] on the Standard toolbar

Or

♦ Press [**Ctrl**]-[**Z**].

If you undo something by mistake, and want to redo it:

♦ Click the **Redo** tool [icon] on the Standard toolbar.

3.6 Margins and orientation

Margins are the white space between the edge of the paper and the text/data area at the top, bottom, left and right of each page.

Orientation describes the way up that a sheet of paper is. The orientation can be portrait (tall) or landscape (wide).

You can easily change the margins and/or orientation of the pages in your file using the **Page Setup** dialog box.

1 Open the **File** menu and choose **Page Setup...**

♦ Word – select the **Margins** tab, set the margins and/or orientation as required.

♦ Excel and Access – select the **Margins** tab for the margins and the **Page** tab for the orientation.

♦ PowerPoint – use the **Page Setup** dialog box to specify the paper size and orientation.

2 Click **OK**.

3.7 Spelling and grammar

To help you produce accurate work, you can use the proofing tools to check the spelling and grammar in a file.

Check that you are using the correct dictionary for your proofing. In the UK, you would normally want to use the English (UK) dictionary rather than the English (US) dictionary.

To check/set the default dictionary:

* Open the **Tools** menu, choose **Language**, then **Set Language...** to display the **Language** dialog box. The default dictionary will be highlighted.

To change the default language:

1 Select the language required in the **Language** dialog box.

2 Click **Default...**

3 Click **OK** at the prompt.

Checking Spelling and grammar as you type

You can let the application check your spelling and grammar as you work (Word and PowerPoint), or run a spell check at a time that suits you (all applications). Check as you type is operational by default – if it isn't on your system, someone has switched it off.

To deal with spelling errors:

Words that aren't recognized will have a red, wavy underline. To find out what Word or PowerPoint suggests as an alternative, right-click on the highlighted word.

* If you wish to change the word to one of those listed, click on the word that you want to use in the shortcut menu.

* If you choose **Ignore All**, the word will not be highlighted again in the document in this working session.

* If you choose **Add**, the word will be added to the dictionary, and recognized as a correctly spelt word from now on.

To deal with grammatical errors:

Any words, phrases or sentences that have unusual capitalization or aren't grammatically correct will have a grey wavy underline. When you right-click on the error, the application will display the problem, and suggest a remedy if it can. You can choose whether to change your text to that suggested or ignore the suggestion.

Checking Spelling and Grammar when you are ready

You can easily check your spelling and grammar at any time using the **Spelling and Grammar** tool on the Standard toolbar.

• Click the **Spelling and Grammar** tool ▨ to start the check.

The application will check the spelling and grammar in your file. Respond to the prompts as you see fit. When the checking is complete, a prompt will appear to tell you so.

• Click OK to return to your file.

3.8 Font formatting

One way of enhancing your text is to apply font formatting to it. Font formatting can be applied to individual characters in your file. The most commonly used options have tools on the Formatting toolbar – others can be found in the **Format > Font** (Word, PowerPoint and Access) or **Format > Cells** (Excel) dialog box. The Formatting toolbar varies a little from application to application – this one is from Word. The formatting options discussed here are available in all Office applications.

To format text or data as you type it in:

1 Switch on the formatting option(s) required.

2 Type in text or data.

3 Switch off or change the formatting option.

To apply or change the formatting of existing text or data:

1 Select the text or data.

2 Switch the formatting option required on or off, or apply an additional format, e.g

• To switch bold on or off, click the **Bold** tool ▨ .

• To switch italic on or off, click the **Italic** tool ▨ .

• To switch underline on or off, click the **Underline** tool ▨ .

Font styles, size and colour

The font style, size and colour are also easily changed.

To change the style of font:

1 Click the drop-down arrow by the **Font** tool `Times New Roman` on the Formatting toolbar.

2 Scroll through the list of fonts and select the font you want.

3 Click on it.

To change the size of font:

1 Click the drop-down arrow by the **Font Size** tool `12` on the Formatting toolbar.

2 Scroll through the list of sizes and select a suitable one.

3 Click on it.

To change the colour of font:

1 Click the drop-down arrow by the **Font Color** tool on the Formatting toolbar to display the Font Color toolbar.

2 Select the colour you want to use.

Format Painter

If you need to apply the same formatting to different pieces of text or cells throughout your file, you can use the Format Painter.

1 Select some text or data that has been formatted using the options you want to apply to other text.

2 Click the **Format Painter** tool .

3 Drag over the text you want to 'paint' the formatting on to.

♦ If you want to paint the formats onto several separate pieces of text, double-click on the Format Painter to lock it. When you have finished, click the tool again to unlock it.

3.9 Paragraph/cell formatting

The default paragraph (Word/PowerPoint) or cell (Excel/Access) formatting options give you left-aligned text, with single line spacing. If this is not the formatting you require you can change it.

To apply formatting to a paragraph or cell as you type:

1 Set the formatting option required.

2 Enter your text.

To apply formatting to existing text:

1 Select the text or cell(s).

2 Apply the formatting required.

Alignment

To centre a paragraph, or text or data within a cell:

- Click the **Centre** tool ▦ on the Formatting toolbar.

To justify a paragraph (or paragraphs):

- Click the **Justify** tool ▦ on the Formatting toolbar.

To right-align a paragraph (or paragraphs):

- Click the **Align Right** tool ▦ on the Formatting toolbar.

To left-align a paragraph (or paragraphs):

- Click the **Align Left** tool ▦ on the Formatting toolbar.

Borders and shading

These paragraph or cell formatting options can be very useful when it comes to emphasizing areas in your file.

To place a border around or between your paragraph(s) or cell(s):

1 Select the paragraph(s) or cell(s).

2 Click the drop-down arrow beside the **Borders** tool to display the options.

3 Select the border required.

To remove a border from your paragraph(s) or cells:

1 Select the paragraph(s) or cell(s).

2 Display the Borders toolbar.

3 Click the **No Border** tool ▦.

There are more options in the **Borders and Shading** dialog box, including an outside border with a Box, Shadow or 3-D setting.

1 Display the **Format** menu and choose **Borders and Shading...** (Word) or choose **Cells** then go to the **Border** tab (Excel).

2 Experiment with the options.

3 Click **OK** or **Cancel** (to accept or abandon your changes).

To switch individual borders (left, right, top or bottom) on and off, click the border tools in the Preview pane, or the lines around the edges of the example in the Preview pane.

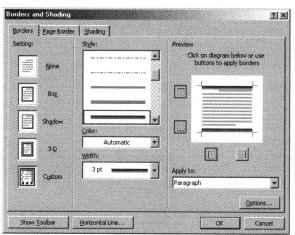

In Excel, border options are on the **Border** tab, and shading options on the **Patterns** tab of the Format Cells dialog box.

To format an individual border, click on its line in the Preview pane then pick a style and colour.

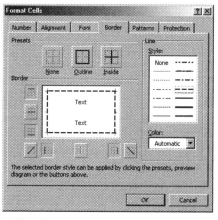

You can choose a shading effect for your paragraph(s) or cell(s). Select the **Shading** tab in the **Borders and Shading** dialog box in Word, or the **Patterns** tab in the **Format Cells** dialog box in Excel, and explore the options.

3.10 Find and Replace

The Find and Replace commands can be useful when working with longer files. **Find** allows you to locate specific text or data quickly. **Replace** enables you to find the specified text and replace it with other text – selectively or globally.

Find specified text:

1 Open the **Edit** menu and choose **Find...** (or press [**Ctrl**]-[**F**]) to display the **Find and Replace** dialog box.

2 On the **Find** tab, enter the text that you are looking for.

3 Click the **More...** button (in Word) or the **Options...** button (in Excel) if you wish to display the search options.

4 Select the options as required.

5 Click **Find Next**.

6 Continue to click **Find Next** until you have located the text.

7 Click **Cancel** to close the dialog box.

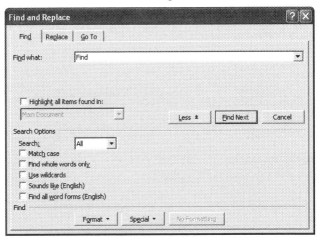

Replace can be a very useful tool – especially if you've spelt a name wrong throughout a file!

1 Open the **Find and Replace** dialog box ([**Ctrl**]-[**F**]).

2 Select the **Replace** tab.

3 Enter the text you want to find in the **Find what:** field.

4 Specify any options and formatting as necessary.

5 Enter the text to replace it with in the **Replace with:** field.

6 Specify any options and formatting as necessary.

7 Click **Find Next**.

• The first occurrence of the text will be highlighted.

8 Click **Replace** to replace this one occurrence, then click **Find Next** again.

Or

• Click **Replace All** to replace all occurrences automatically.

• Experiment with the options and use the dialog box Help button as necessary to explore this feature fully.

Be very careful when using Replace All – it may replace something that you didn't anticipate. Particular danger spots are numbers, where the number may be tucked away in a date, sum of money, address, etc.

3.11 Drawings

You can easily draw shapes and create images in your files using the Drawing toolbar. If it isn't displayed, you need to display it.

• Click the Drawing tool ▨ on the Standard toolbar.

Drawing Canvas

A Drawing Canvas is placed around drawing objects when you create them. In Word, you can create the Drawing Canvas, then add your objects to it, or insert the first object in your drawing and let Word automatically create the Drawing Canvas around it.

To create a Drawing Canvas:

1 Place the insertion point where you want the drawing.

2 Open the **Insert** menu.

3 Choose **Picture**.

4 Select **New Drawing**.

5 Create your drawing objects on the canvas.

Or

1 Select one of the drawing tools.

2 Click, or click and drag to position the object.

• A Drawing Canvas is placed around the object and the Drawing Canvas toolbar is displayed, in Word.

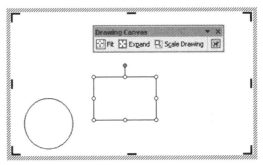

Drawing Canvas toolbar options

Fit resizes the Drawing Canvas to fit neatly around the objects.

Expand makes the Drawing Canvas bigger.

Scale Drawing resizes/scales the Drawing Canvas and the objects within it (handles appear around the Drawing Canvas that you can drag to scale).

Text Wrapping specifies how the text in your document wraps around your drawing.

To align or distribute objects on your canvas:

1 Select the objects that you want to align or distribute.

2 Click the **Draw** tool on the **Drawing** toolbar.

3 Select **Align or Distribute**.

4 Choose an option.

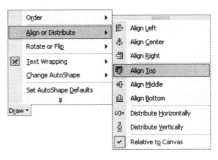

To format the Drawing Canvas:

1 Select the Drawing Canvas.

2 Open the **Format** menu.

3 Choose **Drawing Canvas**.

To draw an object, position the insertion point where you want your drawing to appear and do one of the following:

To draw a line, arrow, rectangle or oval:

1 Click the line, arrow, rectangle or oval tool on the Drawing toolbar.

2 Click and drag, where you want your shape.

To draw a square or circle:

1 Select the rectangle or oval tool on the Drawing toolbar.

2 Click at the position you want the shape.

3 Hold down [**Shift**] and drag on a corner handle to make the shape larger or smaller.

To enter an AutoShape:

1 Click the **AutoShapes** tool on the Drawing toolbar.

2 Pick a category.

3 Select a shape.

4 Click to place your shape, then drag a handle to set its size.

To add a text box:

1 Select the **Text Box** tool.

2 Click at the position you want the text box.

3 Type in your text.

4 Click outside the text box.

Editing drawn objects

If a drawing object is selected it has handles at each corner/along each side (squares). A selected object can be moved, resized or deleted. You can change the line styles or add a fill colour or special effect using the tools on the Drawing toolbar.

To move a shape:

◆ Place the mouse pointer within the shape and click and drag.

To resize a shape:

- Click on it then drag on a handle.

To delete a shape:

- Click on it then press [**Delete**].

To change line style:

- Click the **Line Style** tool and choose a style.

To change line colour:

- Click the arrow beside the **Line Color** tool and pick one.

To change the fill colour:

- Click the arrow beside the **Fill Color** tool and choose a colour.

To add a shadow:

- Click the **Shadow** tool and select an effect.

To add a 3-D effect:

- Click the **3-D effect** tool and choose from the options.

WordArt

WordArt gives you the option of creating special text effects.

1 Click the **Insert WordArt** tool ◢ on the Drawing toolbar.

2 Select a WordArt style from the Gallery and click **OK**.

3 At the **Edit WordArt Text** dialog box, enter (and format) the text then click **OK**.

4 Adjust the shape of your WordArt object as required.

The WordArt toolbar

- Experiment with the tools to see the effects they produce.

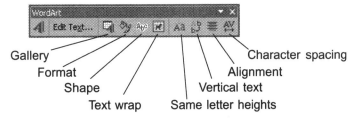

3.12 Pictures

Microsoft Office gives you access to lots of clip art. If you have Internet access, you'll also find many more clips on-line.

To insert clip art:

1 Click the **Insert Clip Art** tool  on the Drawing toolbar.

2 Leave the **Search text** box empty in the Task Pane to display all clips, or, enter a keyword to look for something specific.

3 Set your Search options, e.g. specify the collections and media file types (for clip art, search *All collections* in the **Search in** box, and choose *Clip Art* from the **Results should be** options).

4 Click **Search**.

5 Scroll through the list of clips displayed.

6 Click on the one that you want to use.

7 Close the Task Pane.

♦ The clip can be resized, moved or deleted using the same techniques as with drawings.

The clips that you insert into your document can be formatted in a number of ways – the best thing to do is experiment.

When a clip is selected the Picture toolbar is displayed. You can use the toolbar to modify your picture.

Working from left to right on the toolbar:

Insert Picture inserts a picture from file rather than from the Microsoft Gallery.

Color – *Automatic* is the default. *Greyscale* converts the colours to shades of grey. *Black and white* converts it to black and white only. *Washout* converts it to a pale low contrast picture that you can place behind text to create a watermark.

More Contrast increases the contrast.

Less Contrast decreases the contrast.

More Brightness increases the brightness.

Less Brightness decreases the brightness.

Crop lets you trim the edges of the clip. To crop a picture:

1 Click the **Crop** tool.

2 Drag a resizing handle to crop the bits you don't want.

Rotate Left – turns the picture through 90°.

Compress Picture – allows you to reduce the file size.

Line Style – puts lines around the picture, or changes the line style.

Text Wrapping allows you to specify how you want your text to wrap around your picture.

Format Picture opens the **Format Picture** dialog box where you have access to even more formatting options.

Set Transparent Color – makes one colour transparent. This only works on bitmaps, GIFs and similar image formats. After clicking this, click on a part of the picture with the colour you want to make transparent.

Reset Picture returns the clip to its original state.

You can also edit the inserted clip art, e.g. change the colours.

1 Right-click on the picture.

2 Select **Edit Picture**.

3 The individual objects that make up the picture can now be selected.

4 Double-click on any object to open its **Format** dialog box.

5 Format the object as required and click **OK**.

6 Click outside the picture when finished.

If you have pictures on disk that are not in the Gallery (perhaps a scanned photograph), you can insert them into your document.

To insert a picture from a file:

1 Open the **Insert** menu.

2 Select **Picture**.

3 Choose **From File...**

4 Locate the file to insert – browse the folders on your system.

5 Select the file and click **Insert**.

3.13 Zoom

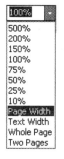

Most files are displayed on your screen at 100% zoom – full size. You can zoom in on your file to get a closer look, or zoom out so that more of the file is displayed on the screen at any one time.

1 Click the drop-down arrow beside the **Zoom** tool.

2 Select the percentage zoom required.

3.14 Toolbars

Standard and Formatting toolbars: Row sharing

If you don't want the Standard and Formatting toolbar to share one row, you can switch off the option that enables this feature. The Standard and Formatting toolbars can then be positioned on two rows – the Standard above the Formatting one.

To toggle the row-sharing option:

1 Click the drop-down arrow at the right of the Standard or Formatting toolbar.

2 Choose **Show Buttons in One Row** or **Show Buttons in Two Rows** as required.

Showing and hiding toolbars

Some toolbars appear and disappear automatically as you work in an application. The Picture toolbar appears when a picture is selected, the WordArt toolbar appears when a WordArt object is selected.

You can opt to show or hide toolbars whenever you want to use the tools on them. Provided you have at least one toolbar displayed, you can use the shortcut method to show or hide any toolbar.

1 Right-click on a toolbar.

♦ Any toolbars that are displayed have a tick beside their name.

2 Click on the name of the toolbar that you wish to show or hide.

If no toolbars are displayed, you can use the **View** menu to show them again.

1 Open the **View** menu and choose **Toolbars**.

2 Click on the one that you want to show.

Using either of these methods, you can show or hide one toolbar at a time. If you want to change the display status of several toolbars at once, it may be quicker to use the **Customize** dialog box.

1 Right-click on a toolbar.

Or

* Open the **View** menu and choose **Toolbars**.

2 Click **Customize...**

3 On the **Toolbars** tab, select or deselect the toolbars as required (a tick means they are displayed).

4 Click **Close**.

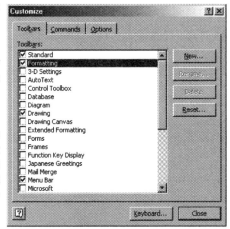

Moving toolbars

Toolbars can be positioned anywhere on your screen. There are four docking areas – at the top, bottom, left and right of your screen, and your toolbars can be placed in any of them. You can also leave your toolbar floating in the document area if you prefer.

The Standard and Formatting toolbars are normally displayed along the top of your screen, docked side by side, sharing one row.

To move a toolbar if it is docked:

1 Point to the two raised lines at its left edge (if it is docked at the top or bottom) or top edge (if it is at the left or right).

2 Drag and drop the toolbar where you want it.

To move a floating toolbar:

1 Point to its Title bar.

2 Drag and drop the toolbar to the position you want it in.

3.15 Keyboard shortcuts

Some keyboard shortcuts are common to most applications, and it can therefore save you quite a bit of time in the long run if you learn and use them. Try the Ctrl alphabet!

Ctrl with	Effect
A	Select all
B	Bold
C	Copy
D	Depends upon the application: Font dialog box (Word); Fill down (Excel); Duplicate (PowerPoint);
E	Centre align
F	Find
G	Go to
H	Replace
I	Italics
J	Justify
K	Insert hyperlink
L	Left align
M	Left indent (Word)
N	New file
O	Open file
P	Print file
Q	Remove paragraph formatting (Word)
R	Replace
S	Save file
T	Hanging indent (Word)
U	Underline
V	Paste
W	Close active window
X	Cut
Y	Repeat the last action
Z	Undo

Summary

This chapter discusses features that can by used in any of the applications in Office. These features included:

- Opening and closing and application
- Online Help
- File handling – New, Open, Save, Save As, Preview, Print and Close
- Delete, Cut, Copy and Paste
- Margins and orientation
- Spell and grammar checker
- Font Formatting
- Paragraph/cell formatting
- Find and Replace
- Drawing toolbar
- Clip art and pictures
- Zoom
- Show, hide and move toolbars
- Keyboard shortcuts

04

word processing

In this chapter you will learn

- basic Word skills
- about page layout
- how to use templates and styles
- about tables and graphs
- how to create a mail merge

4.1 Starting Word

When you start Word, a new blank document is displayed on the screen. Its name – *Document1* – is displayed on the title bar.

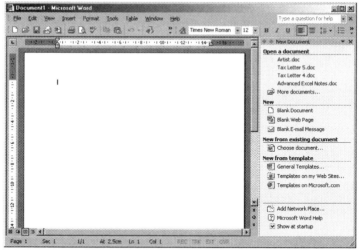

Each new document that you create during a session in Word is given a temporary name following the *Document1* format. Your second document will be called *Document2*, the next *Document3* and so on. These names should be considered temporary – you will save your document and give it a meaningful name instead of the temporary name assigned by Word.

If you want to start typing into a new blank document, simply click the Close button at the top right of the Task Pane to remove it from the screen and give you a larger document area.

The insertion point – the flashing vertical bar – is in the top left of the text area on the first page. You're ready to start – just type!

Things to remember when entering text into your document:

- DO NOT press [**Enter**] at the end of each line. If a sentence is going to run onto a new line, let it – the text will be wrapped automatically at the end of the line.

- DO press [**Enter**] at the end of short lines, e.g. after lines in an address or after the last line in a paragraph, or to create one or more extra blank lines between headings or in the signature block at the end of a letter.

4.2 Moving the insertion point

When you need to fix a mistake, the first thing you have to do is place the insertion point next to the error. If necessary, use the scroll bars to bring the text you want to edit into view.

There are several different ways of moving the insertion point.

Using the mouse:

1 Position the I-beam (the name given to pointer when it is over a text area) at the place you want the insertion point.

2 Click the left mouse button.

Using the keyboard:

*   To move a character or line at a time press [←], [→], [↑] or [↓].
*   To move right or left one word press [**Ctrl**] and [←] or [→].
*   To move up or down one paragraph press [Ctrl] [↑] or [↓].
*   To move to the start of the line press [**Home**].
*   To move to the end of the line press [**End**].
*   To move to the start of the document press [**Ctrl**]-[**Home**].
*   To move to the end of the document press [**Ctrl**]-[**End**].

4.3 Editing

To insert new text:

1 Position the insertion point where you want the new text.

2 Type in your new text.

To delete existing text:

1 Position the insertion point next to the character that you want to delete.

2 To delete the character to the left, press the backspace key [←].

Or

*   To delete the character to the *right,* press [Delete].
*   Both [←] and [**Delete**] repeat – if you hold them down they will zoom through your text removing it much quicker than you could type it in, so be careful with them!

To insert a new paragraph:

◆ Position the insertion point where the paragraph break should be and press [**Enter**] – twice if you want to leave a blank line.

To join two paragraphs:

◆ Delete the [**Enter**] characters between the paragraphs.

Overtype

You can type over existing text, replacing the old text with the new in one operation, instead of deleting then entering the new. Press [**Insert**] to switch Overtype mode on and off.

◆ When Overtype mode is on, the text on the Overtype button OVR on the Status bar is black.

1 Switch on Overtype mode – press [**Insert**].

2 Position the insertion point within some existing text and type – watch carefully to see what happens – the old text will be replaced with the new text you enter.

3 Switch Overtype mode off again – press [**Insert**].

Page breaks

As you type in your text a page break is inserted automatically when you reach the end of your page. However, if you want a page break to occur at a specific point, e.g. at the end of a chapter or topic, you can easily insert a forced page break.

1 Position the insertion point where the page break should be inserted.

2 Press [**Ctrl**]-[**Enter**].

4.4 Selection techniques

Selection techniques are *very* important in Word. You need to use them if you want to:

◆ Copy or move text within a document.

◆ Copy or move text from one document to another.

◆ Change the formatting of existing text.

♦ Quickly delete large chunks of text.

There are several ways to select text in Word – try some out and use whatever seems easiest for you.

Using the mouse

♦ To select any amount of text, click and drag over it, or click at start of text, hold down [**Shift**], click at end of text.

♦ To select a word, double-click on it.

♦ To select a sentence, hold down [**Ctrl**] and click anywhere within the sentence.

♦ To select a paragraph, double-click to the left of the paragraph *or* triple-click anywhere within it.

♦ To select the whole document, triple-click in the left margin.

To deselect any unit of text:

♦ Click anywhere within your text.

Using the keyboard

♦ To select a character or line at a time, hold [**Shift**] down and press [←], [→], [↑] or [↓].

♦ To select right or left, a word at a time, hold [**Shift**] down, hold [**Ctrl**] down and press [←] or [→].

♦ To select up or down a paragraph at a time, hold [**Shift**] down, hold [**Ctrl**] down and press [↑] or [↓].

♦ To select to the end of the line press [**Shift**]-[**End**].

♦ To select to the beginning of the line press [**Shift**]-[**Home**].

♦ To select to the beginning of the document press [**Shift**]-[**Ctrl**]-[**Home**].

♦ To select to the end of the document press [**Shift**]-[**Ctrl**]-[**End**].

♦ To select the whole document press [**Ctrl**]-[**A**].

To deselect any unit of text:

♦ Press one of the arrow keys.

Don't be afraid to experiment with the different selection techniques. Many of the keyboard ones are much more efficient than the usual click and drag method.

4.5 Word options

When Word is initially set up on your computer, the default file location for documents is normally the *My Documents* folder.

Other options, e.g. unit of measure (for margins/ruler), whether or not to show the Task Pane on start-up, and user information (name/initials) are also set.

You can easily change any of these from the **Options** dialog box.

To change the options currently set:

1 Open the **Tools** menu.

2 Click **Options...**

3 Explore the tabs to see the current options.

4 Edit any as required.

5 Click **OK**.

Changing the default directory (for Save/Open operations):

1 Open the **Options...** dialog box.

2 Display the **File Locations** tab.

3 Highlight **File Type, Documents...** and click **Modify**.

4 Select the folder that you want to become the default folder for Save/Open operations.

5 Click **OK**.

To change the units of measurement:

1 Open the **Options...** dialog box.

2 Display the **General** tab.

3 Select the **Measurement Units** required.

4 Click **OK**.

To update user information:

1 Open the **Options...** dialog box.

2 Display the **User Information** tab.

3 Update the name/initials as required.

4 Click **OK**.

4.6 Special characters and symbols

Most of the characters you want to type into your document are available through the keyboard. However, there may be times when you want a character that is not on the keyboard. You may find it in the **Symbols** dialog box. Here are some examples:

   € ® ¾ ë

1 Position the insertion point where you want the character.

2 Open the **Insert** menu.

3 Choose **Symbol**.

4 Select the font from which you wish to select a character (you'll need to spend time exploring the fonts you have available).

5 Select a character – click on it.

6 Click **Insert**.

7 Click **Close** to close the dialog box.

4.7 View options

When working in a document, there are several view options. These control how the document looks on the screen – not how it will print out. You will usually work in Normal or Print Layout view.

Normal view

Normal view is the default, and the most efficient for entering, editing and formatting text. The page layout is simplified – margins, headers and footers, multiple columns, pictures, etc. are not displayed.

To change to Normal view:

♦ Open the **View** menu and choose **Normal**.

Or

♦ Click the Normal view tool at the bottom left of the screen.

Print Layout view

In this view you can see where your objects will be positioned on the page. Your margins are displayed (and any headers or footers within them), and pictures, drawings, multiple columns, etc. are all displayed in their true position on the page. Print Layout view is useful if you are working with headers and footers, altering your margins, working in columns, or are combining text and graphics and wish to see how they will be placed relative to each other.

To change to Print Layout view:

◆ Open the **View** menu and choose **Print Layout**.

Or

◆ Click the Print Layout view tool at the bottom left of the screen.

Show/hide white space

The top and bottom margins are usually displayed as white space in Print Layout view. You can opt to show or hide this white space.

1 Go into Print Layout view (if necessary).

2 Move the mouse pointer to the top or bottom edge of a page.

3 Click when the **Show White Space** or **Hide White Space** prompt appears.

◆ The other view options are Web Layout and Outline view. You don't need to know how to use these views at this stage, but have a look at them if you wish. Open one of your documents and experiment with the view options.

Non-printing characters

Non-printing characters are those which affect the layout of your text, but don't print. For example, the characters inserted when you press the spacebar, [Enter] key, tab or non-breaking space character.

You can toggle the display of non-printing characters – you can opt to have them displayed on your screen or hidden. Either way they *do not* print – they are non-printing.

◆ To toggle the display of non-printing characters, use the Show/hide tool on the Standard toolbar.

4.8 Font formatting

Standard formatting routines are used when formatting characters in Word (see section 3.8). Explore the Font dialog box to see what other font formatting options are available.

1 Open the **Format** menu and choose **Font**.
2 Select the **Font** tab.
3 Choose the effects you want – a preview of your selection is displayed in the Preview window.
4 Click **OK** to apply the effects to your text, or **Cancel** to return to your document without making any changes.

In particular, explore the **Effects** on the Font tab, e.g. superscript, subscript, shadow, outline, emboss, etc. and the underline options in the Underline field.

4.9 Paragraph formatting

Some formatting options are applied only to complete paragraphs, regardless of whether it consists of a few words or several lines. A paragraph is created in Word each time you press the [**Enter**] key.

The Alignment and basic Borders and Shading options were covered in the Common Skills chapter (section 3.9).

Borders and Shading

You can add and remove borders using the Border tool on the Formatting toolbar, or the Tables and Borders toolbar.

◆ Click the Tables and Borders tool ▦ to toggle the display of the **Tables and Borders** toolbar.

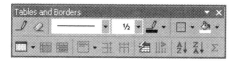

To add borders to your text, paragraph or table:

1 Select the text, paragraph(s) or table cells.
2 Choose a **Line Style** from the options.
3 Pick a **Line Weight** from those available.

4 Select a colour from the **Border Color** options.

5 Use the **Border** tool to specify where you want the border.

Line spacing

Initially, your line spacing is set to single. You can
set different spacing using the **Line Spacing** tool.

1 Select the text that you wish to change.

2 Click the drop-down arrow beside the **Line
Spacing** tool.

3 Click on the Line Spacing option required.

To apply the most recently used line spacing option, simply click
the **Line Spacing** tool (not the drop-down arrow).

Keyboard shortcuts

You can quickly set line spacing using keyboard shortcuts.
Double line spacing: [Ctrl]-[2]; 1½ line spacing: [Ctrl]-[5];
single line spacing: [Ctrl]-[1].

If you wish to set line spacing to a measurement other than one of
those listed, click **More...** and specify your requirements in the
Line Spacing field in the **Format Paragraph** dialog box (you can
also access this dialog box from the **Format** menu).

Paragraph spacing

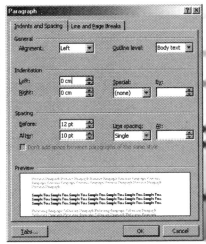

You can control the amount
of space before and after a
paragraph in the **Format
Paragraphs** dialog box. This
option is useful if you want
a specific amount of space
above/below, or you wish to
leave a space between paragraphs without having to
press [**Enter**] twice.

1 Open the **Format** and
choose **Paragraph** to
open the dialog box.

2 Set the spacing before and/or after the selected paragraph(s) – use the split arrows to adjust the values, or type the settings into the fields.

3 Click **OK**.

Bulleted and numbered lists

You can add bullets or numbers automatically to your paragraphs.

1 Click the Bullets tool 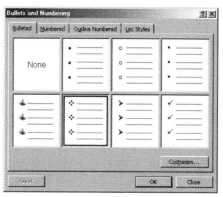 to switch bullets on or off.

2 Click the Numbering tool on to switch the bullets or numbers on or off.

To change the bullet or number style:

1 Select the paragraphs.

2 Open the **Format** menu and choose **Bullets and Numbering**.

3 Select the **Bulleted** or **Numbered** tab in the dialog box.

4 Choose a bullet or numbering option from those displayed.

5 Click **OK**.

Indents

Paragraphs normally run the full width of the typing line – from the left to the right margin. As you enter your text, it extends along the line until it reaches the right margin and then it automatically wraps to the next line (unless you press [**Enter**]).

To increase the indent of a paragraph from the left margin:

♦ Click the **Increase Indent** tool on the Formatting toolbar.

To decrease the indent of a paragraph from the left margin:

♦ Click the **Decrease Indent** tool on the Formatting toolbar.

Indent markers

You can also use the ruler to set your indents. The ruler must be displayed along the top of your text area – if it's not, open the **View** menu and choose **Ruler** to display it.

The indent markers are the two triangles and the small rectangle at the left of the ruler, and the small triangle at the right. Drag the appropriate marker along the ruler to set the indent.

To adjust the indent of:

◆ *The first line in the paragraph from the left margin*, drag the top triangle at the left edge of the ruler.

◆ *All other lines (except the first) in the paragraph from the left margin*, drag the bottom triangle at the left edge.

◆ *All lines in the paragraph from the left margin*, drag the rectangle below the two triangles at the left.

◆ *All lines in the paragraph from the right margin*, drag the triangle at the right edge of the ruler.

To improve accuracy when setting indents using the ruler, you can display the exact position of your indent as you drag it along.

◆ Hold [**Alt**] down while you click and drag.

Alternatively

1 Open the **Format** menu and choose **Paragraph…**

2 Select the **Indents and Spacing** tab.

3 Set the indents required in the **Indentation** fields.

4 Click **OK**.

Tabs

Tabs are used to align your text. If you want, say, a list of names and telephone numbers you can use tabs to align each column.

The default tabs are set every 1.27 cm (half-inch) along the ruler – the small dark grey marks along the bottom of the ruler indicate their positions.

Each time you press [**Tab**] the insertion point jumps to the next tab position. The default tabs have left alignment – when you enter your text the left edge will align with the tab position.

Tabs can be aligned to the left, right, centre or a decimal point.

Alignment	Effect	Possible use
Left	The left edge is at tab	Any text or numbers
Right	The right edge is at tab	Numbers you want to line up on the unit
Centre	Centred under the tab	Anything
Decimal	Decimal point under tab	Numbers you want to line up on the decimal point

To set a tab using the ruler:

1 Select the type of tab – click the button to the left of the ruler until you've got the required alignment.

2 Point to the lower half of the ruler and click – your tab is set.

To move a tab:

♦ Drag it along the ruler to its correct position.

To delete a tab:

♦ Drag it *down* off the ruler, and drop it.

To set tabs in the Tabs dialog box:

1 Open the **Format** menu and choose **Tabs**.

2 Enter the **Tab stop** position.

3 Select the alignment.

4 Click **Set**.

5 Set a leader line or dots style if required.

6 Repeat until all your tabs are set, then click **OK**.

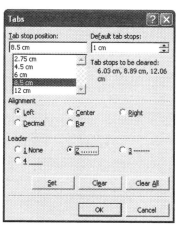

Hyphenation

Hyphenation can help to make line lengths similar throughout a document. It gives a document a more professional look by limiting the amount of white space left at the end of each line, and between words when the text is justified.

The easiest way to ensure that your text is hyphenated appropriately is to have the Automatic hyphenation option turned on.

1 Open the **Tools** menu, choose **Language**, then **Hyphenation**.

2 Select the **Automatically hyphenate document** checkbox, and set the other fields as required.

3 Click **OK**.

Manual line break

A manual line break ends the current line of text and continues your text on the next line. It *does not* start a new paragraph, but simply inserts a line break within the current paragraph.

◆ To insert a manual line break, hold [**Shift**] and press [**Enter**].

Manual line breaks are useful at the end of lines that use tabs to align columns of text or figures. If you separate the lines in your tabbed layout with manual line breaks, then move the tabs when the insertion point is within your tabbed layout, the whole column moves, not just the line with the insertion point (as would be the case if you created a new paragraph at the end of the line).

4.10 Print Preview and Print

See section 3.4 for standard preview and print information.

When you preview your file a full page is displayed at a time. You can zoom in and out to read the text, and you can edit your text.

Print Preview toolbar

The Print Preview window has its own toolbar which can be used to control the display of your document on the screen.

Experiment with the tools to see what effect they have. From left to right on the toolbar, your have:

Print

If you are happy with the appearance of your document, and want to print it from the preview window, click the **Print** tool on the Print Preview toolbar. One copy of the document will be printed.

Magnifier

If you move your pointer over your page in Print Preview, you will notice it looks like a magnifying glass with a + on it.

* Position the pointer over your page and click the left button and you will be zoomed in and out of your document.

Editing text in Print Preview

If you zoom in on your text, and notice something that you want to change, you can edit your document in print preview.

* Click the **Magnifier** tool on the Print Preview toolbar.

The insertion point will appear. Edit your document and click the **Magnifier** tool again so that you can zoom in and out.

One Page

Click this to display one page on the screen at a time.

Multiple Pages

This tool drops down a grid. Click and drag over it to indicate the number of pages you want to display at one time.

Zoom

Sets the percentage of magnification on your document.

View Ruler

Toggles the display of the vertical and horizontal rulers.

Shrink to Fit

If a small amount of text appears on the last page of your document you may be able to reduce the number of pages by clicking this tool. Word decreases the size of each font used in the document to get the text to fit on to one page less.

Full Screen

This removes most of the toolbars, menu bar, title bar, etc. to get a 'clean screen' display. To return the screen to normal, click **Close**

Full Screen on the Full Screen toolbar or press [**Esc**].

Close Preview

Exits Print Preview and returns you to your document.

Context Sensitive Help

Click this, then click on a tool, scroll bar, ruler, etc. to get a brief description of its function. Once you've read the information, click anywhere on your screen to close the information box.

Moving through your document in Print Preview

If you have more than one page in your document, you can scroll through the pages in Print Preview to check them. To do this:

◆ Click the arrow up or arrow down at the top or bottom of the vertical scroll bar.

Or

◆ Click the **Previous Page** or **Next Page** buttons at the bottom of the vertical scroll bar.

Print

If you don't want to print the whole document, you can specify the pages to print in the **Print** dialog box. You can also specify the number of copies from the dialog box.

1 Open the **File** menu and choose **Print**.

2 Select the **Page range** – *All*, *Current page* (the one the insertion point is in) or *Pages* e.g.1,2,4-7,12.

◆ If you have selected some text before displaying the dialog box, the **Selection** option is active so that you can print this text.

3 Set the number of copies required – usually 1.

4 Click **OK**.

4.11 Templates

A *template* is a pattern on which a document is based. You have probably been creating documents using the *Blank Document* template – this is used when you click the **New** tool. The document created has an A4 paper size, portrait orientation, 2.54 cm (1 inch) top and bottom margin, 3.17 cm (1.25 inch) left and right margin and single line spacing. Paragraph and character styles that are part of the *Blank Document* template are available in the style list on the Formatting toolbar (see section 4.12).

Word comes with other templates. You should look through them as you may find some of them useful. There are templates for letters, memos, fax, résumés (CV) and other types of document.

To create a document using a different Word template:

1 Open the **File** menu and choose **New** to display the New Document Task Pane.

2 Select **General Templates…** from the **New from template** list.

3 Explore the tabs in the **Templates** dialog box.

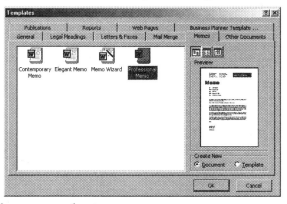

4 Choose a template.

5 Click **OK**.

Explore the document that you have created. Check out the layout – notice that some templates, e.g. memo and fax, include areas for your company name, address, telephone/fax number, etc.

Many of the documents created using a Word template include details on how to use and complete the new document. In the main, you just follow the instructions on the screen. Select and replace pieces of text that are used to prompt you for your own details e.g. 'Enter company name here'.

With other prompts, just do as you're told – click in the highlighted area and enter your information.

Your own templates

If you have a standard layout, e.g. your own memo or letterhead, you should save the basic layout and formatting as a template.

To create your own template:

1 Create a new document based on a selected template and customize it as required – enter your company name, address, etc.

Or

♦ Create a new blank document and set up the layout, standard text, etc. required for your template.

♦ Page Setup (section 4.13), headers and footers (4.14), styles (4.12), etc. can all be set up to suit your requirements.

2 Open the **File** menu and choose **Save As…**

3 In the **Save as type** field, choose *Document Template*.

4 Select the folder in which you wish to store your template – choose the *Templates* folder or one of its subfolders.

5 Give your template a name and click **Save**.

Try out some of the templates on your system – they could help you produce a very professional looking document easily.

4.12 Styles

As an alternative to formatting text manually (using the Formatting toolbar or the dialog boxes) you could format it using a set of formatting options that have already been set up in a *style*. Each document you create in Word will have several styles set up. The text you have entered into your documents has been formatted using the *Normal* style – Times New Roman, size 12, left aligned.

To display the available styles:

♦ Click the drop-down arrow by the **Style** box on the Formatting toolbar to see the styles in the current document.

Many styles are already set up in Word – far more than those in the Style list. Different styles are recorded in the various templates and are automatically available when you create a document using these.

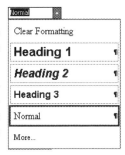

To apply a style to new text:

1 Click the drop-down arrow by the **Style** box to open the list.

2 Select the style you want to use – click on it.

3 Type in your text.

4 Press [**Enter**].

Some sample styles

Heading 1 – Arial, size 14, bold, left aligned, spacing before 12 pt, spacing after 3 pt

Heading 2 – Arial, size 12, bold, italic, left aligned, spacing before 12 pt, spacing after 3 pt

Heading 3 – Arial, size 12, left aligned, spacing before 12 pt, spacing after 3 pt

Normal – Times New Roman, size 12, spacing before and after 0 pt

When you press [**Enter**] after each of the Heading styles, the style used for the *following paragraph* returns to **Normal** automatically.

To apply a style to existing text:

1 Select the text you want to apply a style to.

2 Click the drop-down arrow by the **Style** box to open the list.

3 Select the style you want to use.

> Styles are magic! They'll help you achieve a consistent look within and across your documents. You can also set up your own styles – check out the online Help.

4.13 Page Setup

You can change the page setup for all or part of your document. Initially, documents based on the default template consist of one *section*. If you select *Apply to: This Point Forward* when changing the page layout as discussed below, Word creates a new section in your document. Each can have different margins, orientation, page size, etc. If a document has more than one section the **Apply to:** field in the **Page Setup** dialog box has three options – *Whole document*, *This point forward* and *This section* – so that you can modify the layout of existing sections. The number of the section that the insertion point is currently in is displayed at the left of the Status Bar, beside the page number.

Margins

To change the margin setting:

1 Open the **File** menu and choose **Page Setup…**

2 Select the **Margins** tab.

3 Edit the margin fields as required.

4 Specify the area of your document you want to apply the changes to in the **Apply to:** field.

5 Click **OK**.

Orientation

The orientation of a page can be *Portrait* or *Landscape*. The default is Portrait. You can change the orientation for all of your document or for part of it as required.

To change orientation:

1 Open the **File** menu and choose **Page Setup…**

2 Select the **Margins** tab.

3 Choose the orientation required.

4 Specify the area of your document you want to apply the changes to in the **Apply to:** field.

5 Click **OK**.

Page size

If you are not printing onto A4 size paper, you may need to change the page size setting so that Word can format the pages correctly.

To change the page size:

1 Open the **File** menu and choose **Page Setup…**

2 Select the **Paper** tab.

3 Choose the **Paper Size** required.

4 Specify the area of your document you want to apply the changes to in the **Apply to:** field.

5 Click **OK**.

4.14 Headers/footers

Headers and footers can be displayed at the top and bottom of each page and can contain things like page numbers, the author's name, the file name or the date that the document was created.

To insert a header or footer:

1 Open the **View** menu.

2 Choose **Header and Footer**.

The insertion point moves to the header area and the **Header and Footer** toolbar is displayed. The main document text is dimmed.

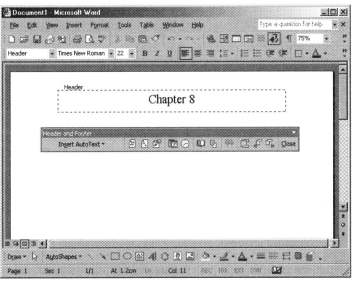

The header and footer area has a centre tab set in the middle of the line and a right tab at the end. You can use these to help you position your text and/or page numbers. You can type any text you wish into the header and footer areas. Use the tabs to help you position the insertion point as necessary.

You can format your text in the same way as you format text in the main document area.

Use the tools on the Header and Footer toolbar to insert fields that will be completed and updated automatically by Word.

* You can also number your pages by choosing **Page Numbers...** from the **Insert** menu and setting the options in the dialog box.

Always use headers and footers for text or numbers that you want on every page. *NEVER* type them into the main text area!

Header and footer tools

Insert AutoText	Insert file name, author name, etc.
Insert Page Number	Inserts automatic page numbering
Insert Number of Pages	Inserts the total number of pages in the document
Format Page Number	Choose alternative formats for your page numbers
Insert Date	Inserts the date that the document is printed
Insert Time	Inserts the time that the document is printed
Page Setup	Displays the dialog box so you can set up header and footer options
Show/hide document text	Toggles the display of the document text
Same as Previous	Makes/breaks link between headers and footers in different sections of a document
Switch Between Header And Footer	Switches between the header and footer area
Show Previous	Displays the previous header or footer in document (if document divided into sections)
Show Next	Displays the next header or footer in document (if document divided into sections)
Close	Returns you to your document

4.15 Tables

Tables are used to lay out text and data. Tables consist of rows and columns. Where a row and column intersect, we have a cell.

Row — Column — Cell

To create a table:

1 Place the insertion point where you want your table to appear.

2 Click the **Insert Table** tool on the Standard toolbar.

3 Click and drag over the grid that appears until you get the number of rows and columns required.

4 Release the button – you have an empty table on your page.

You can move around your table using the keyboard or the mouse.

• Press [**Tab**] to move forward to the next cell.

• Press [**Shift**]-[**Tab**] to move back to the previous cell.

Or

• Click in the cell you want to move to.

To select cells in a table:

• Click and drag over the cells you want to select.

Or

1 Click in the corner cell of the range of cells you want to select.

2 Point to the cell in the diagonally opposite corner.

3 Hold [**Shift**] down and click.

To select a column:

• Click the top gridline or border of the column you want to select (you should get a black arrow pointing downwards).

• To select several adjacent columns, drag along the top border.

To select a row:

• Click to the **left** of the row you want to select.

• To select several adjacent rows, drag up or down the row selector area (to the left of the table).

Click to select column

Click to select row

To select a cell:

◆ Click just inside the **left** edge of the cell.

Other things to note:

◆ When entering text into a cell, you will find that it automatically wraps once the text reaches the right edge, and the row deepens to accommodate the text (provided you have spaces between the words, or you pressed [**Enter**]).

◆ If you press [**Tab**] when the insertion point is in the last cell in the last row of your table, a new row is created.

◆ You can format your cells, or text within the cells, as normal, e.g. with bold, italic, colour, size, alignment (the text is aligned *within* the cell), borders and shading, etc.

Column width

In most cases, you won't want all your columns to be the same width – it depends what you're entering. You can easily change the column width. There are several methods you might like to try. The insertion point must be within a table when using these.

AutoFit

You must have some text or data in your columns to give AutoFit something to work on.

◆ Double-click the border or gridline to the right of the column whose width you want to change.

Hotel	Address	Prices
Old Mill Inn	24 Mill Lane Melrose	Dinner £35: Single Room £30: Double Room £45
Kathy's Kitchen	12 High Street Duns	Lunch from £6. High Tea from £10

You will also find a number of AutoFit options in the **Table** menu. Experiment with them to see how the different options work.

To adjust manually:

1 Position the pointer over the gridline or border to the right of the column.

2 Click and drag the border or gridline as required.

Or

• Click and drag the **Move Table Column** marker (on the ruler) which is above the right border of the column.

You can also adjust the column width from the **Table Properties** dialog box.

To display the dialog box:

1 Open the **Table** menu and choose **Table Properties...**

2 Select the **Column** tab.

3 Set the width and click **OK**.

Row Height

You can adjust the row height in a similar way to column width.

To adjust manually:

1 Position the pointer over the border or gridline below the row you want to adjust.

2 Click and drag the border or gridline as required.

Or

• Click and drag the Row Marker on the vertical ruler.

You can also set the height in the **Table Properties** dialog box.

1 Open the **Table** menu and choose **Table Properties...**

2 Select the **Row** tab.

3 Set the height required and click **OK**.

Insert and delete rows and columns

To insert a row:

1 Select the row that will be above the new row.

2 Right-click on the selected area.

3 Choose **Insert Rows** from the shortcut menu.

To insert a column:

1 Select the column that will be to the right of the new column.

2 Right-click on the selected area.

3 Choose **Insert Columns** from the shortcut menu.

You may find that you have to adjust the width of your columns to accommodate the new ones.

To delete a row or column:

1 Select the row or column that you want to delete.

2 Right-click on the selected area.

3 Select **Delete Rows** or **Delete columns**.

To delete an entire table:

1 Place the insertion point anywhere inside the table.

2 Open the **Table** menu and choose **Delete**.

3 Select **Table**.

• If you select some cells, or the whole table, and press [**Delete**], the *contents* are deleted, but the cells, or table, remain in place.

Table Autoformat

You can of course format the text, data and cells within your table using the Formatting toolbar and the dialog boxes. There are also some table *Autoformats* that you can use to quickly format a table.

1 Click anywhere inside your table.

2 Choose **Table Autoformat** from the **Table** menu.

3 Select an **Autoformat** from the dialog box.

4 Select or deselect the checkboxes as required until you have the formatting options required.

5 Click **Apply**.

• Experiment with the tools on the Tables and Borders toolbar when working with your tables.

4.16 Mail merge

You can combine the text and/or layout of a standard document (e.g. a letter) with a set of variables (usually names and addresses) to produce personalized documents using mail merge. The letters that you receive from banks, building societies and sales organizations, etc. promoting services and products, and personalized with your name and address, are often the result of a mail merge.

Mail merge jargon

The **main document** is the document that contains the layout, standard text and field names that point to the data source.

The **data source** is the file that contains the records you require for your mail merge – perhaps a name and address file. It is usually in a table layout – it could be a Word file or an Access or Excel table. We will create a data source in Word.

A **record** is a set of information on one item in the data source.

A **field** is a piece of data within a record. Title, surname, first name, telephone number, etc. would be held in separate fields.

A **field name** is the name used to identify a field.

The **result document** is the document produced when you combine the records in the data source with the main document.

There are three steps involved in mail merge:

1 Creating the **main document**.

2 Creating and/or locating the **data source**.

3 Merging the two to produce the **result document**.

If you are going to mail merge a letter, type and save the letter first. If you wish to use an existing file as the main document, open it. Use the Mail Merge Wizard to step you through the process.

The document and the data source

1 Open the **Tools** menu.

2 Choose **Letters and Mailings**, then **Mail Merge Wizard**.

3 The **Mail Merge** Task Pane will be displayed.

4 At step 1, choose *Letters* as the document type, and click **Next**.

5 At step 2, choose *Use Current Document* – we are using the document that we have open, then click **Next**.

6 At step 3, choose *Type a new list*, then click **Create…** to set up the data source.

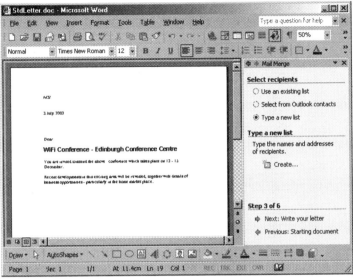

7 Add details of your address list into the data file.

8 Click **New Entry** when you have finished one record and want to enter another one.

9 Click **Close** when you have finished.

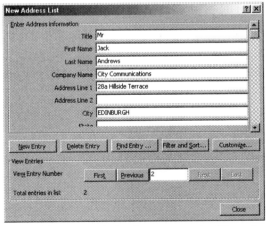

10 At the **Save Address List** dialog box, name the file and save it, then click **Next**. The list is saved as an Access database.

11 Click **OK** at the **Mail Merge Recipient** dialog box.

12 Click **Next** to go to step 4.

To set up the Main document:

1 At step 4, *Write your letter* type the letter (if needed).

2 Place the insertion point where you want the address and click **Address Block** in the Task Pane.

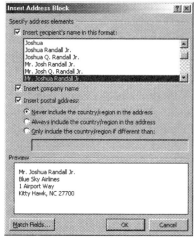

3 Select the options for your address and click **OK**.

4 Place the insertion point where you want the salutation and click **Greeting Line** – edit the set up and click **OK**.

5 If you have any more fields to insert, position the insertion point as necessary and click **More items…**

6 Insert the fields required.

7 Close the dialog box when you've finished.

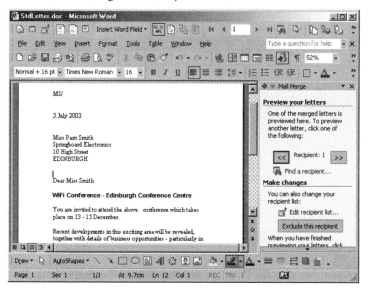

To produce the Result document:

1 Click **Next: Preview your letters**, to see the results.

2 At step 5, use the buttons near the top of the Task Pane to move through your letters and check the layout.

3 If the layout is wrong, click **Previous** at the bottom of the Task Pane to return to step 4 and adjust the layout.

4 Click **Next: Complete the merge** at the bottom of the Task Pane to get to the final step.

5 If all letters are fine, click **Print...** to print them out.

6 If you wish to edit individual letters, click **Edit individual letters...** to create a result document that you can edit, save and print.

7 Close the Task Pane when you've finished.

Mail Merge toolbar

If you are familiar with mail merge, or you prefer not to use the Wizard, you can use the Mail Merge toolbar. This appears automatically if you work through the Wizard. You can use its tools to work with your Mail Merge document.

From left to right:

♦ **Main document setup** sets a document as a main document.

♦ **Open Data Source** opens your name and address list – usually an Access database or Outlook Contact List.

♦ **Mail Merge Recipients** sorts and/or specifies recipients from the data source.

♦ **Insert Address Block/Greeting Line/Merge Field** insert field names that link the main document to the data source information.

♦ **Insert Word Field** helps you control how Word merges in data. See 'About Mail Merge Field Codes' in the online Help.

♦ **View Merged Data** displays the results for the current record.

♦ **Highlight Merge Fields** shades the merge fields.

♦ **Match Fields** allows you to select the field name in your data source that corresponds to the information that Word expects.

- **Propagate Labels** generates a sheet of labels from one definition.
- **First/Previous/Next/Last Record** all move through the records.
- **Find Entry** locates records where specified criteria are met.
- **Check for Errors** checks the field names and Word fields.
- **Merge to New Document/Printer/Email/Fax** are all destinations for the result document.

Editing the data source

Once opened, the data source can be edited. New entries may be added, obsolete ones removed, or existing records can be edited.

1 Open the Data Source file (if necessary).

2 Click **Mail Merge Recipients**.

3 Click **Edit...**

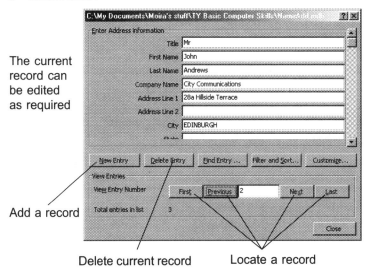

The current record can be edited as required

Add a record

Delete current record   Locate a record

4 Edit, delete or add new records as required.

5 Click **Close**.

Labels

This time try creating labels, using the Mail Merge toolbar.

1 Create a new blank document and display the Mail Merge toolbar (if necessary).

2 Click **Main Document Setup**.

3 Select **Labels**.

4 Choose a standard address label and click **OK**.

5 Click the **Open Data Source** tool and open your data file.

6 In the first label, click the **Insert Address Block** tool, or use **Insert Merge Fields** to build your label up field by field.

7 Once the first label is complete, click the **Propagate Label** tool.

8 Click **View Merged Data** to display your result document (or **Merge to a New Document** or **Printer** as required).

4.17 Charts

To create a chart:

1 Open the **Insert** menu.

2 Select **Picture**, and then click **Chart**.

♦ The chart datasheet window will appear

3 Enter the data that you want to create a chart from into the datasheet (replace the sample data with your own).

4 When you've finished setting up your chart, click on your document, outside the chart area, to return to your document.

5 To edit an existing chart, double-click on it. The datasheet, Charting toolbar and **Chart** menu will appear again.

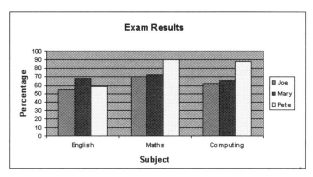

To insert or delete rows or columns:

1 Select the row or column in the datasheet (click the row number or column letter).

2 Right-click on the selected area.

3 Click **Insert** or **Delete** as necessary.

When you are working on a chart, you will see that the Standard toolbar displays several tools for manipulating charts. Explore these tools and experiment with them to see their effects.

You will also notice a **Chart** menu in the Menu bar – explore its options. There are two options that you should try out.

• **Chart Type** – opens a dialog box that gives you access to a greater range of chart types and options than the **Chart Type** tool on the Charting toolbar.

• **Chart Options** – opens a dialog box that lets you add a chart title, add axis titles, move the legend, etc.

You can resize and move a chart just as you can any other object, e.g. a picture, in your document.

1 Click on the chart once to select it, then…

2 Drag a resize handle (in each corner and half way along each side) to make the chart bigger or smaller.

Or

3 Point to the middle of the chart and drag to move it.

To format an individual object within your chart:

1 Double-click on the chart to display the datasheet, Chart toolbar and **Chart** menu.

2 Double-click on the object you want to format.

3 Select the options from the dialog box, then click **OK**.

• See 5.19, 7.7 and 7.8 for more information on charts – they are very similar in Excel and PowerPoint.

4.18 Importing objects

To import a spreadsheet or chart into Word:

1 Open the **Insert** menu and choose **File…**

2 Locate and select the workbook that contains the data or chart that you want to import and click **Insert**.

3 Choose **Entire Workbook**, or click the drop-down arrow and select the sheet required.

4 Complete the **Name or Cell Range** field as required.

5 Click **OK**.

* Data is inserted as a Word table and can be edited in Word using table handling features.

You can also copy text, data, graphics, charts, etc. from one Office application to another using simple copy and paste techniques.

1 Launch Word and the application you want to copy from.

2 Select the object, text or data you want to copy.

3 Click the **Copy** tool on the Standard toolbar.

4 Switch to Word.

5 Place the insertion point where you want the object, text or data to appear.

6 Click the **Paste** tool.

* If you copy and paste data from Excel, the data is displayed in a Word table.

4.19 Keyboard shortcuts

Keystrokes	Effect
[Shift]-[Ctrl]-[+]	Superscript
[Ctrl][=]	Subscript
[Ctrl]-[D]	Display Font dialog box
[Shift]-[F3]	Change case
[Shift]-[Ctrl]-[C]	Copy formatting
[Shift]-[Ctrl]-[V]	Paste formatting
[Ctrl]-[Shift]-[Spacebar]	Create a non-breaking space
[Ctrl]-[1]	Single line spacing
[Ctrl]-[5]	One and a half line spacing
[Ctrl]-[2]	Double line spacing
[F5] or [Ctrl]-[G]	Display the Find and Replace dialog box (Go To tab)
[Shift]-[Enter]	Manual line break
[Ctrl]-[Enter]	Manual page break

Summary

This chapter has discussed the features in Word that you should be able to use. We have discussed:

* Navigating and editing in Word

* View options

* Font and paragraph formatting options including bullets, numbering, tabs, indents, etc.

* Templates

* Styles

* Page Setup

* Headers and footers

* Tables

* Mail Merge

* Charts

* Importing data from other applications

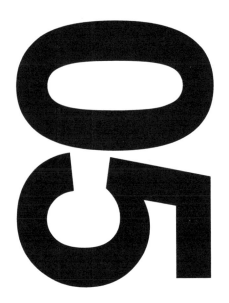

05

spreadsheets

In this chapter you will learn

- how to enter data in Excel
- how to adjust the size of rows and columns
- about writing formulae
- how to sort data
- how to create charts

5.1 Workbooks and worksheets

When working in Excel, the files that you work with are called *workbooks*. Each workbook consists of a number of *worksheets* (the default number is three). You can add more worksheets to a workbook if necessary, or remove any that you don't need.

Related data is usually best kept on separate worksheets in the same workbook – this makes it easier to find and manage data.

When you start Excel, you are presented with a new workbook displaying a blank worksheet. *If the workbook window is maximized, the workbook and the application share one Title bar containing the application and workbook names.*

Worksheets

The worksheet tabs appear at the bottom left of your screen – to the left of the horizontal scrollbar.

To move from one sheet to another in your workbook:

♦ Click the sheet tab of the sheet you want to work on.

If you can't see all the sheet tabs in the bar, use the navigation buttons to the left of the tabs to scroll the other tabs into view.

To insert a new worksheet:

1 Select the worksheet (click on its tab) you want to have to the *right* of the new one.

2 Open the **Insert** menu and choose **Worksheet**.

♦ A new worksheet will appear to the left of the selected one.

If your workbook contains too many sheets you can easily delete any that you don't need.

To delete a worksheet:

1 Select the sheet you want to delete.

2 Open the **Edit** menu and choose **Delete Sheet**.

Be careful when deleting worksheets – **Undo** will not restore them!

By default, worksheets are named *Sheet1*, *Sheet2*, etc. You can rename the worksheets with a name that actually means something.

To rename a worksheet:

1 Double-click on the sheet tab.

2 Type in the name you want to use.

3 Press [**Enter**] or click anywhere on the worksheet.

You can easily move or copy a worksheet within the workbook, or to another open workbook.

To move or copy a worksheet:

1 Select the worksheet.

2 Open the **Edit** menu and choose **Move or Copy Sheet…**

3 Drop down the **To book:** list and choose the book to move or copy it to.

4 Select a sheet – this doesn't apply if you choose *(new book)* in the **To book:** field.

5 Tick **Create a copy** if you want to make a copy of the sheet, not move it.

6 Click **OK** – the sheet will be inserted before the selected one.

♦ If you move or copy your worksheet to a new book, remember to save the new workbook.

To move the worksheet within a workbook:

1 Click and drag the sheet tab along the tabs to its new position.

To copy the worksheet within a workbook:

2 Click on the sheet tab, hold [**Ctrl**] down and drag the tab to the required position.

5.2 Spreadsheet jargon

Before going any further, you need to learn some spreadsheet jargon. There's nothing difficult about it – once you know what it means!

The worksheet area consists of *rows*, *columns* and *cells*. Rows are identified by the numbers displayed down the left side of the worksheet area. Row 6 is highlighted in the illustration opposite. There are lots of rows on a worksheet – 65,536 in fact!

Columns are identified by letters displayed along the top of the worksheet. Column C is highlighted in the illustration. After Z, columns are labelled AA to AZ, then BA to BZ, and so on to IV, giving 256 columns in all.

Address of active cell (Name box)

Formula bar

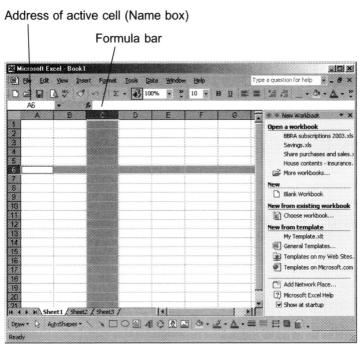

Where a row and column intersect you have a cell. Cells are identified by addresses which consists of the column letter followed by the row number.

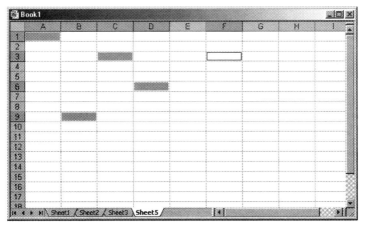

Cells are identified by their column letter and row number. Cell A1, B9, C3, D6 and F3 are highlighted here.

Text, data, formulas and functions

The cells in a worksheet can contain text, numeric data, formulas or functions.

Text is used for titles or narrative to describe the figures you are presenting – worksheet titles, column headings and row labels will usually be text entries.

Numeric data means the figures that appear in your worksheet. The data may be entered through the keyboard, or it may be generated as the result of a calculation.

Formulas are used to perform calculations on the data in your worksheet. They are used to add the value in one cell to that in another or multiply the values in different cells, etc. Some of your formulas will be very basic while others may be quite complex.

Functions are predefined formulas that perform simple or complex calculations on your data. There are many different kinds of functions set up in Excel – statistical, logical, financial, database, engineering – and many more. You're bound to find some useful ones, whatever type of data you work with.

5.3 Moving around your worksheet

Before you can enter anything into a cell, you must make the cell you want to work on *active*. To make a single cell active, you must select it. You can easily move onto any cell (thus making it active) using either the keyboard or the mouse.

The active cell has a dark border. The address of the active cell appears in the Name Box to the left of the Formula bar.

To navigate with the mouse:

• Scroll the sheet to bring the cell into view if necessary and click into the cell to make it the active cell.

Navigation with the keyboard

To go to the next cell:

• Use the [←], [→], [↑] and [↓] arrows on the keyboard.

To move onto the cell directly below:

• Press [**Enter**].

To go to a specific cell address:

1 Press [F5].

2 Enter the address of the cell you want to go to in the Reference field of the **Go To** dialog box.

3 Click **OK**.

To go to cell A1:

* Press [Ctrl]-[Home].

To move to the end of your work area:

* Press [Ctrl]-[End].

Check out 'Keyboard shortcuts' in the online Help to see if there are any others that you would find useful.

5.4 Selection techniques

You will find that you often work on more than one cell at a time in Excel. You may need to format a group of cells in a particular way or copy or move a group of cells, or apply a function to a group of cells.

A group of cells is called a *range*. Cell ranges are identified by using the first cell address followed by the last cell address in the group of cells you wish to work on e.g. A1:A7, C3:D12, F5:H7 are highlighted in the picture below.

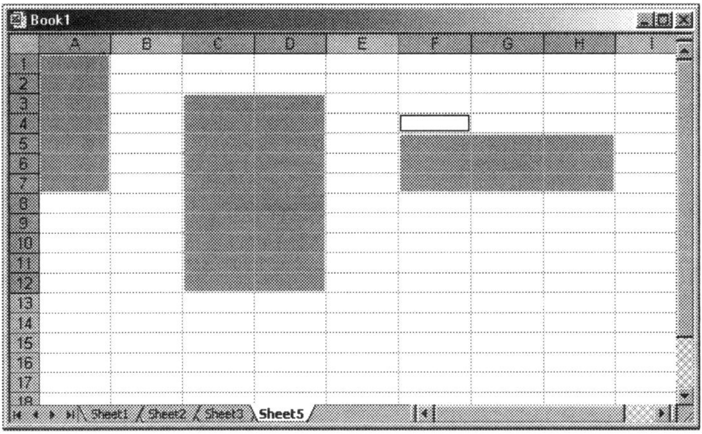

To select a group of adjacent cells:

• Click and drag with the mouse.

Or

1 Select the cell in one corner of the range.

2 Hold [**Shift**] and select the cell in the diagonally opposite corner.

To select a row:

• Click the row number to the left of the row you want to select.

To select several adjacent rows:

• Click and drag down over the numbers to the left of the rows.

To select a column:

• Click the column letter at the top of the column.

To select several adjacent columns:

• Click and drag across the letters at the top of the columns.

To select the whole worksheet:

• Click the box at the top left of the row and column headers.

To select a range of *non*-adjacent cells:

1 Click on one of the cells you want to select.

2 Hold [**Ctrl**] down and click on each of the other cells.

To de-select a range of cells:

• Click on any cell in your worksheet or press an arrow key.

5.5 Entering text and numeric data

Entering text or data into your worksheet is easy.

1 Select the cell you want to enter text or data into.

2 Type in the text or data – it will appear in the Formula bar as well as in the active cell.

3 Press [**Enter**] or click the 'tick' button to the left of the Formula bar when you've completed the cell.

Things to note when entering text:

• Text automatically aligns to the left of a cell.

• Text that doesn't fit into a single cell will 'spill over' into the cell to the right if that one is empty.

- Excess text will not be displayed if the cell to the right is not empty. Widen the column (see section 5.6), reduce the font size or use a more compact number format to display it all.

Things to note when entering numeric data

- Numeric data automatically aligns to the right of a cell.

- If a cell displays ######## instead of the figures you will need to change the number format or adjust the column width to show all the data.

	A	B	C	D	E	F	G
	Book1						
1	Sales figures for 1st quarter						
2		January	February	March	Total		
3	Ann	£75,000.00	£52,000.00	£45,000.00	########		
4	Robert	£60,000.00	£65,000.00	£55,000.00	########		
5	Gill	£55,000.00	£70,000.00	£65,000.00	########		
6	Jackie	£86,000.00	£65,000.00	£75,000.00	########		
7	Jim	£90,000.00	£80,000.00	£80,000.00	########		
8							
9							
10							
11							
12							
13							
14							
15							
16							
17							

Sheet1 \ **Sheet3** / Sheet5 /

Editing text and numeric data

If you make an error when entering your work, you can fix things by deleting, replacing or editing the contents of the cell.

To delete the contents:

1 Select the cell (or cells) whose contents you want to erase.

2 Press [**Delete**].

To replace the contents of a cell:

1 Select the cell whose contents you want to replace.

2 Type in the text or data that should be in the cell.

To edit the contents of a cell:

1 Select the cell whose contents you want to edit.

2 Click in the Formula bar to place the insertion point in it.

Or

- Double-click in the cell – this places the insertion point in it.

3 Edit the cell contents as required.

4 Press [**Enter**] when you've finished editing.

5.6 Adjusting columns and rows

All the columns in a worksheet are the same width unless you change them.

To change the width of a column manually:

- Drag the vertical line (in the heading row) to the right of the column, e.g. to change the width of column B drag the vertical line between columns B and C.

To adjust the column width automatically:

- Double-click the vertical line to the right of the column.

To change the height of a row manually:

- Click and drag the horizontal line below the number of the row whose height you want to adjust, e.g. to change the height of row 5 drag the horizontal line between rows 5 and 6.

To adjust the row height automatically:

- Double-click the line below the number of the row.

You can also adjust the column width or row height from the **Format** menu.

If you need extra rows or columns in the middle of your working area, you can easily insert them as necessary. You can also delete rows or columns that you don't require.

To insert a row:

1 Select the row that will go *below* the row you are inserting.

2 Right-click within the selected area.

3 Choose **Insert** from the pop-up menu.

To insert a column:

1 Select the column that will go *to the right* of the column you are inserting.

2 Right-click within the selected area.

3 Choose **Insert** from the pop-up menu.

To delete a row or column:

1 Select the row or column you wish to delete.

2 Right-click within the selected area.

3 Choose **Delete**.

To add or delete several rows or columns at once:

1 Click and drag in the row or column label area to indicate the number of rows or columns you want to insert or delete.

2 Right-click within the selected area.

3 Choose **Insert** or **Delete** as required.

5.7 Fitting text into cells

When entering text into cells you might want to try some other formatting options to help you display your work effectively. These options can be used on any cells, but may be particularly effective on column headings. Options include: merged cells, text wrap, shrink to fit, orientation and vertical alignment.

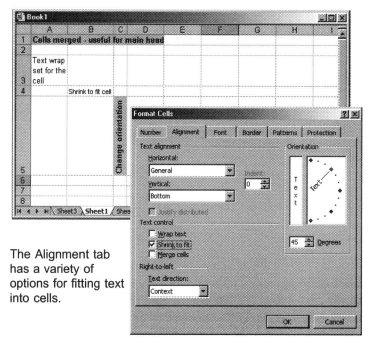

The Alignment tab has a variety of options for fitting text into cells.

These options can all be found in the **Format Cells** dialog box, on the **Alignment** tab.

1 Select the cells you want to format.

2 Open the **Format** menu and choose **Cells…**

3 Select the **Alignment** tab.

4 Specify the option(s) required.

5 Click **OK**.

◆ You may need to adjust the row height or column width manually if it doesn't adjust automatically to accommodate the alignment options you choose.

5.8 Number formats

When entering currency values into a worksheet, you will usually want the appropriate symbol to precede the figure, e.g. a £ symbol or €.

If you want the £ symbol in front of a figure you can either:

◆ Format the cells to display the entry in a currency format.

Or

◆ Enter the £ symbol through the keyboard.

If you enter your figures through the numeric keypad, it's probably easiest to format the cells to display the figures as currency.

You can format cells *before* or *after* you have entered your text or data.

To display the figures in currency format:

1 Select the cells you want to format.

2 Click the **Currency** tool ▨ on the **Formatting** toolbar.

On UK keyboards, the keyboard shortcut for the € is [**Alt Gr**]+[**4**]. If this doesn't work on your keyboard, check out "How to type the Euro sign" in the online Help.

The Formatting toolbar has other tools for formatting numbers – **Percent, Comma, Increase** and **Decrease Decimal**. Other formats can be found on the **Number** tab of the **Format Cells** dialog box.

To apply a format from the Format Cells dialog box:

1 Select the cells you want to format.

2 Open the **Format** menu and choose **Cells...**

3 Select the **Number** tab.

4 Choose a category from the list, e.g. Currency.

5 Complete the dialog box as required, e.g. you may want to select a different symbol if the currency isn't £.

6 Click **OK**.

5.9 Freeze/unfreeze headings

Many of the worksheets you create will be considerably larger than will fit on to your computer screen. You will need to scroll vertically and horizontally to display the data you want to work with.

When you scroll through your worksheet, the column and row headings will disappear off your screen as the other data appears. This is often very inconvenient, as you need to see the column headings or row labels to make sense of your data. In a situation like this you can *freeze* part of your worksheet window so that it doesn't move, and then scroll the unfrozen part of your window.

To freeze rows or columns:

1 Select the row below the ones you want to freeze.

Or

♦ Select the column to the right of the ones you want to freeze.

Or

♦ Select the cell below the rows and to the right of the columns that you want to freeze.

2 Open the **Window** menu.

3 Choose **Freeze Panes**.

When you scroll through your worksheet horizontally, the frozen column(s)remain in view. When you scroll through it vertically the frozen row(s) will remain in view when the other data scrolls.

To unfreeze panes:

1 Open the **Window** menu.

2 Choose **Unfreeze Panes**.

5.10 Split screen

There will also be times when you want to compare the data on one part of your worksheet with that on another – but the data ranges are in separate areas of the worksheet. When this happens, you should *split* your screen so that you can scroll each part independently, to bring the data you require into view.

If you look carefully at the top of the vertical scroll bar (above the up arrow), or to the right of the horizontal scroll bar (outside the right arrow), you will notice the *split box*. You must use the split boxes to split your screen.

To split your screen horizontally:

• Drag the split box at the top of the vertical scroll bar down to where you want your split to be.

To split your screen vertically:

• Drag the split box at the right of the horizontal scroll bar along to where you want your split to be.

When your screen is split, you can scroll each pane independently to view the data you want to see.

To remove a split:

• Double-click the split.

5.11 Formulas

Any cell which will contain a figure that has been calculated using other entries in your worksheet should have a formula. (Do *not* do your calculations on a calculator, then type in the answer!)

Formulas allow you to add, subtract, multiply, divide and work out percentages of the values in cells. The main operators are:

+	Add	–	Subtract	/	Divide
*	Multiply	%	Percentage		

Formula examples

=A7/B6	Divide the figure in A7 by the figure in B6
=D22*12	Multiply the figure in D22 by 12
=C7*25%	Calculate 25% of the figure in C7

Order of precedence

If there is a mixture of operators, Excel deals with multiplication and division *before* it deals with the addition and subtraction, e.g.

=A4+C7*D7   Multiply C7 by D7, and add the answer to A4

Parentheses (brackets)

Some formulas can become quite long and complicated. If you want to force the order in which a formula is worked out, or just make a long formula easier to read, you must use parentheses ( ).

In the example below, the problem within each set of parentheses is solved *before* working through the formula.

=((A1+B2)*C3)) - (D4/E5)

Add A1 to B2   we'll call this XX

Multiply XX by C3   we'll call this YY

Divide D4 by E5   we'll call this ZZ

Subtract ZZ from YY

Remember the BODMAS rule – Brackets over division, multiplication, addition then subtraction!

Entering formulas

You can enter a formula either by typing it into the Formula bar, or by *pointing* with the mouse. Let's say that you wanted to enter the formula =B4-C4 into cell D4.

1 Select the cell, D4.

2 Type '=' – this tells Excel that the cell contains a formula.

3 Either type 'B4-C4'.

Or

♦ Click on B4 and its reference will be written into the formula, then type '-', and finally click on C4 to get its cell reference.

4 Press [**Enter**].

AutoFill

AutoFill can be used to copy formulas down columns or across rows. In the screenshot, the formula in cell D4 is =B4-C4. We need a similar formula in the other cells in the column.

To complete the cells using AutoFill:

1 Select D4.

2 Position the pointer over the bottom right corner of the cell. The Fill Handle – a small black cross – should appear.

3 Click and drag the black cross over the other *Saving* cells.

	A	B	C	D	E	F	G	H
1	Furniture Sale - everything reduced by 60%							
2								
3	Item	RRP	Sale Price	Saving				
4	Desk	£ 300.00	£ 120.00	£ 180.00				
5	Chair	£ 195.00	£ 78.00					
6	Table	£ 360.00	£ 144.00					
7	Bed	£ 400.00	£ 160.00					
8								
9								
10								

When you release the mouse, the formula in D4 will be copied into the cells you dragged over.

If you click on each cell in the *Saving* column and keep an eye on the Formula bar, you will notice that Excel has automatically changed the cell addresses in the formula *relative* to the position you have copied the formula to.

You can also use AutoFill to automatically generate days of the week, months of the year or dates.

1 Enter 'January', 'Jan', 'Monday' or 'Mon' in any cell.

2 AutoFill it down or across.

To fill with dates:

1 Enter the first date in your series.

2 AutoFill using the *right* mouse button.

3 Select the **Fill** option (*Days*, *Weekdays*, *Months* or *Years*) required from the pop-up menu.

5.12 AutoSum

The worksheet below contains details of monthly sales figures.

To calculate the totals for each sales representative for the quarter, and the total for each month, we could use a formula, e.g. =C4+D4+E4, but the easiest way is to use *AutoSum*.

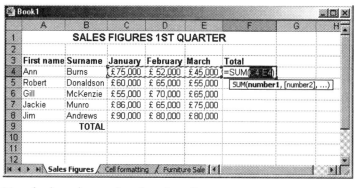

To calculate the totals using AutoSum:

1 Select a cell in which you want a total figure to appear, e.g. the cell that will contain the total sales for the first sales person.

2 Click the AutoSum tool ▒ on the Standard toolbar.

3 The range of cells to be added together will be highlighted. Note that the function appears in the Formula bar.

4 If the suggested range of cells is correct, press [Enter].

Or

• If the suggested range is *not* the range of cells you want to add together, drag over the correct range, and then press [Enter].

5 Use AutoFill to copy the function down or across the other total cells.

If you are totalling rows and columns as in this example, you could use a shortcut that performs all the calculations in one move.

To AutoSum several groups of cells simultaneously:

1 Select all of the rows and columns you want to total, *and* the cells that will contain the results of the AutoSum calculations.

2   Click the AutoSum tool  on the Standard toolbar.

The cells in the rightmost column and bottom row of the selected area will each have the Sum function inserted into them.

You can also use AutoSum to total non-adjacent cells if you wish.

To total non-adjacent cells:

1   Select the cell that will contain the result of the calculation.

2   Click the **AutoSum** tool on the Standard toolbar.

3   Click on the first cell you want to include in the range of cells.

4   Hold [**Ctrl**] down and click on the other cells to be included.

5   Press [**Enter**].

If you prefer to type in the SUM function, start with '=' (equals).

A range of adjacent cells is defined by the address of the first cell, followed by ':', then that of the last cell, e.g. =SUM(B4:B10).

The addresses for non-adjacent cells must be separated by ',' (comma), e.g. =SUM(B4,C6,D9).

5.13 Statistical functions

Statistical functions include minimum, maximum, average, count – and many others. These can be used to display a value from a range of cells.

♦   To return the minimum value from a range use **MIN**.

♦   To return the maximum value from a range use **MAX**.

♦   To return the average value from a range use **AVERAGE**.

♦   To count the number of entries in a range use **COUNT**.

You can use the drop-down list beside the AutoSum tool  to display the functions.

1   Select the cell that the function will go in.

2   Click the drop-down arrow to the right of the AutoSum tool.

3   Select the function. If it is not listed, click **More Functions**, explore the **Insert Function** dialog box and select it from there.

4 Check/amend the cell range as necessary.

5 Click **OK**.

You can also display the **Insert Function** dialog box by clicking the **Insert Function** tool to the left of the Formula bar.

1 Describe what you are trying to do and click **Go**.

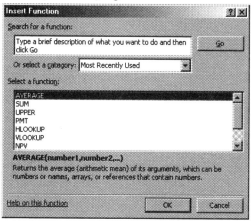

Or

♦ Select a function category, and then select a function.

2 Once you've found the function, select it and click **OK**.

♦ If the function you want has been used recently, it will be listed in the *Most Recently Used* list. If you're not sure what category the function you require is in, select *All* (every function is listed here, in alphabetical order). Minimum, Maximum, Average and Count can be found in the *Statistical* category.

3 Enter the range of cells you want the function to operate on – either drag over the range, or type the cell addresses (minimize the **Function Argument** dialog box – click 🔳 on the right of the function argument field – so you can see your worksheet).

4 Restore the **Function Argument** dialog box – click 🔳 on the right of the function argument field.

5 Click **OK**.

In this example statistical functions have been used to display:

♦ The **lowest** result in each exam (minimum)

♦ The **highest** result in each exam (maximum)

- The **average** mark for each subject (average)
- The **number** of students (count).

	A	B	C	D	E	F
1	Exam Results					
2						
3	Firstname	Surname	Maths	English	Computing	
4	Alison	Anderson	60%	45%	80%	
5	Bill	Andrews	50%	88%	59%	
6	Gavin	Blair	63%	56%	72%	
7	Jill	Blair	50%	80%	76%	
8	Julie	Collins	74%	68%	78%	
9	Paul	Dunsire	30%	60%	95%	
10	Anne	Peterson	70%	68%	74%	
11						
12	Lowest Mark		30%	45%	59%	
13	Highest Mark		74%	88%	95%	
14	Average Mark		57%	66%	76%	
15						
16	Number of students		7			
17						

5.14 View formulas

When setting up your worksheet, it is sometimes useful to display and print the formulas that you have entered into the cells.

To toggle the display of the formulas:

1 Open the **Tools** menu and select **Options…**

2 Select the **View** tab.

3 Select (to show) or deselect (to hide) the *Formulas* checkbox.

4 Click **OK**.

You may need to adjust the column widths to display the whole formula or function in some columns.

	A	B	C	D	E
1	Exam Results				
2					
3	Firstname	Surname	Maths	English	Computing
4	Alison	Anderson	0.6	0.45	0.8
5	Bill	Andrews	0.5	0.88	0.59
6	Gavin	Blair	0.63	0.56	0.72
7	Jill	Blair	0.5	0.8	0.76
8	Julie	Collins	0.74	0.68	0.78
9	Paul	Dunsire	0.3	0.6	0.95
10	Anne	Peterson	0.7	0.68	0.74
11					
12	Lowest Mark		=MIN(C4:C10)	=MIN(D4:D10)	=MIN(E4:E10)
13	Highest Mark		=MAX(C4:C10)	=MAX(D4:D10)	=MAX(E4:E10)
14	Average Mark		=AVERAGE(C4:C10)	=AVERAGE(D4:D10)	=AVERAGE(E4:E10)
15					
16	Number of students		=COUNT(C4:C10)		
17					

* You can print out a copy of your worksheet with the formulas displayed – you may find it useful for reference purposes.

5.15 Sort

The data in your worksheet can be sorted into ascending or descending order. A simple sort is where the data is sorted using the entries in one column only. You can also have more complex sorts, where you can sort on up to three columns at a time.

To perform a simple sort:

1 Select any cell in the column you want to base your sort on.

2 Click the **Sort Ascending** or **Sort Descending** tool on the Standard toolbar.

To perform a multi-level sort:

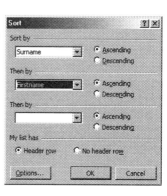

1 Select any cell in the group of cells you want sorted.

2 Open the **Data** menu and choose **Sort...**

3 Select the main sort field from the **Sort by** list.

4 Click **Ascending** or **Descending**.

5 Select the second level sort field from the first **Then by** list, and set its sort order.

6 If necessary, set the third level sort options.

7 Click **OK**.

* By default, Excel assumes your list has a Header row. This is the row that normally contains the column labels or field names. If your list doesn't have a header row, i.e. you want to include the first row in the sort, select the **No header row** option.

5.16 IF function

The IF function is used to return one value if the condition you specify is True, and another value if the condition is False. The values returned can be text, numbers, or the result of a formula.

For example, you might have student end of term exam results in a sheet. If a student has 50% or more in the exam, a pass will be awarded, if less than 50% is achieved, the result is a fail.

Comparison operators

This example uses a *comparison* operator to check if the Total Mark is greater than or equal to 50. The operators include:

=	equal to	<>	not equal to
>	greater than	>=	greater than or equal to
<	less than	<=	less than or equal to

- Enter the data below into a new worksheet

	A	B	C	D	E
1	END OF TERM EXAM RESULTS				
2					
3	Firstname	Surname	Total Mark	Result	
4	Andrew	Borthwick	75		
5	Gill	McLaren	57		
6	Amanda	Mitchell	76		
7	Alison	Peterson	66		
8	Ann	Shaw	42		
9	Peter	Shaw	63		
10	Clare	Stephen	83		
11	Kim	Stephen	79		
12	Gordon	Williamson	39		
13	Jack	Williamson	77		
14					

- To return a Pass or Fail message in the Result column, we need to use a formula based on the IF function.

To enter the function:

1 Select the first cell in the result column.

2 Click **More Functions** on the AutoSum drop-down list.

Or

- Click the **Insert Function** button on the left of the Formula bar.

3 Select the IF function from the list (if it isn't listed, go for **More Functions** – you'll find it in the *Logical* category).

- The **Function Arguments** dialog box is displayed.

4 Enter the condition in the **Logical test** field, e.g. C4>=50.

5 Specify the value if the condition is found to be true. You don't need to type the quotes – Excel will add them automatically.

6 Specify the value if the condition is found to be false.

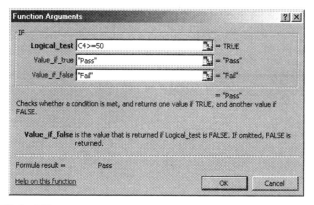

7   Click **OK**.

* AutoFill the formula down the *Result* column. 'Pass' will appear where the condition is true, 'Fail' where it is false.

With the formulas displayed, the worksheet looks like the illustration below.

	A	B	C	D	E
1	END OF 1				
2					
3	Firstname	Surname	Total Mark	Result	
4	Andrew	Borthwick	75	=IF(C4>=50,"Pass","Fail")	
5	Gill	McLaren	57	=IF(C5>=50,"Pass","Fail")	
6	Amanda	Mitchell	76	=IF(C6>=50,"Pass","Fail")	
7	Alison	Peterson	66	=IF(C7>=50,"Pass","Fail")	
8	Ann	Shaw	42	=IF(C8>=50,"Pass","Fail")	
9	Peter	Shaw	63	=IF(C9>=50,"Pass","Fail")	
10	Clare	Stephen	83	=IF(C10>=50,"Pass","Fail")	
11	Kim	Stephen	79	=IF(C11>=50,"Pass","Fail")	
12	Gordon	Williamson	39	=IF(C12>=50,"Pass","Fail")	
13	Jack	Williamson	77	=IF(C13>=50,"Pass","Fail")	
14					

5.17 Relative and absolute cell addresses

You have already noticed that when you AutoFill or copy a formula, the cell addresses used in it change automatically, relative to the position that you copy them to. By default, the cell addresses used in formulas are what we call *relative addresses*.

There will be times when you use a cell address in a formula, and want to copy it down some rows or across some columns, but you don't want the cell address to change relative to its new position.

In this example, we are going to calculate the amount of foreign currency we would get for our holiday spending money (£150). We are going to calculate its value in Euros, Dollars, Kroons (Estonia) and Rupees (India).

	A	B	C	D
1	**Spending money (£)**		**150**	
2				
3		Exchange rate to the £	Value of spending money	
4	Euros	1.38754		
5	Dollars	1.6385		
6	Estonian Kroon	21.715		
7	Indian Rupee	76.89808		
8				

• You could find the current exchange rates on the Internet.

The formula to calculate the value in Euros in cell C4 is **=B4*C1**.

When the formula is copied, we want B4 to become B5 (for Dollars), B6 (for Kroon) and B7 (for Rupee).

We *don't* want C1 (our spending money in £), to change at all.

To stop the cell address changing when we copy it, we must make the cell address *absolute*. An absolute address will not change when the formula containing it is copied or moved.

• An absolute address has a $ sign in front of each co-ordinate that does not change.

You can type the $ sign, or use [F4].

To create absolute addresses in a formula:

1 Select the cell that contains the formula (C4 in this example) – the formula appears in the Formula bar.

2 Click in the Formula bar.

3 Place the insertion point to the *right* of the cell address you want to make absolute (C1).

4 Press [F4] to change the nature of the address. Each time you press [F4] it moves through the absolute addressing options:

$C$1 neither co-ordinate will change

C$1 the column will change if you copy the formula across columns

$C1 the row will change if you copy the formula down rows

C1 both co-ordinates will change relative to its new position.

Your final worksheet should look similar to the one opposite. The first picture displays the formulas (you may have different cell addresses if you have used different rows and columns for your data), the second one shows the results.

	A	B	C
1	Spending mo|		150
2			
3		Exchange rate to the £	Value of spending money
4	Euros	1.38754	=$C$1*B4
5	Dollars	1.6385	=$C$1*B5
6	Estonian Kroon	21.715	=$C$1*B6
7	Indian Rupee	76.89808	=$C$1*B7
8			

	C	D
	:)	150
3	Exchange rate to the £	Value of spending money
4	Euros	1.38754	€ 208.13
5	Dollars	1.6385	$245.78
6	Estonian Kroon	21.715	3,257.25 kr
7	Indian Rupee	76.89808	INR 11,534.71
8		

The currency formats are found in the **Format Cells** dialog box.
Select the **Number** tab, then the **Currency** category. Scroll through
the Symbol list until you find the symbol required.

Common error messages

Error	Probable reason	Solution
######	Column not wide enough	Adjust column width
Value!	A value is of the wrong data type, e.g. text	Put a number in the cell, or amend the cell address
#DIV/0!	You are dividing by a cell that is empty or contains 0	Enter a value in the cell, or amend the cell address
#REF!	The cell referenced has been deleted	Replace #REF! with a valid cell address

Full details of error messages, possible causes and
solutions, are available in the on-line Help.

5.18 Preview, Page Setup and Print

It is very important that the worksheet that you print and distribute is accurate and well presented. You must check the accuracy of each spreadsheet carefully, e.g. spell check the file, check that the data and formulas are correct.

In addition to this, there are several options that you can use to ensure that your worksheet is displayed effectively.

Print Preview

At some stage you will want to print your file. Before sending a worksheet to print, it's a good idea to *preview* it (see section 3.4).

You cannot edit an Excel worksheet in Print Preview. If you want to change something when you see the preview:

1   Click the **Close** tool on the Print Preview toolbar to return to your worksheet.

2   Edit the worksheet as required.

3   Preview again to see how it looks.

Page Setup

The **Page Setup** dialog box can be used to change the orientation, paper size, margins and other aspects of the printed page layout.

Pages are usually printed portrait (rather than landscape).

To change the orientation:

1   From a worksheet, open the **File** menu and choose **Page Setup**.

Or

•   If you are in Print Preview, click **Setup...** on the Print Preview toolbar to open the **Page Setup** dialog box.

2   Select the **Page** tab.

3   Choose an Orientation option – portrait or landscape.

4   Click **OK**.

The default paper size used for printing is A4. You can select an alternative page size if necessary.

To change the paper size:

1   Open the **Page Setup** dialog box and select the **Page** tab.

2   Choose the paper size required from the **Paper size** list.

3   Click **OK**.

To change the margins:

1   Open the **Page Setup** dialog box and select the **Margins** tab.

2   Specify the margins you want to use.

3   Click **OK**.

If your worksheet is more than a page in size, you can specify the number of pages to print it on with the Scaling option. You can also specify whether to print *down then across* or *across then down*.

To change the scaling:

1 Open the **Page Setup** dialog box and select the **Page** tab.

2 In the **Scaling** options, specify the number of pages wide and the number of pages tall you want your worksheet to fit on.

3 Click **OK**.

◆ This option is particularly useful if the last page of your sheet contains only a small amount of data. You can specify that the worksheet print on one page less than it really needs – Excel will scale it down to fit onto that number of pages.

To specify the order of printing:

1 Open the **Page Setup** dialog box and select the **Sheet** tab.

2 In the **Page order** options, select the order required.

3 Click **OK**.

Page breaks

If your worksheet runs to more than one page, Excel will divide it into pages by inserting automatic page breaks. Exactly where the page breaks appear depends on the paper size, margin settings and scaling options you have set. You can set your own page breaks.

To insert a horizontal page break:

1 Select the row *below* where you want the page break.

2 Open the **Insert** menu and click **Page Break**.

To insert a vertical page break:

1 Select the column to the *right* of where you want the page break.

2 Open the **Insert** menu and click **Page Break**.

To move a page break:

1 Open the **View** menu and click **Page Break Preview**.

◆ The first time you go into **Page Break Preview** a prompt appears to tell you how to move the breaks – if you don't want this prompt to appear again, select the checkbox and click **OK**

2 Drag the page break to its new position.

To insert a horizontal and vertical page break at the same time:

1 Select the cell immediately below and to the right of where you want to start a new page.

2 Open the **Insert** menu and click **Page Break**.

To remove a page break:

1 Open the **View** menu and click **Page Break Preview**.

2 Right-click on a cell below a horizontal page break.

Or

◆ Right-click on a cell to the right of the vertical page break.

3 Click **Remove Page Break** on the shortcut menu.

4 Open the **View** menu and click **Normal** to return to your worksheet.

Repeat rows at top of page

If you have a big spreadsheet, with headings that you would like repeated at the top of each page printed, you can use the **Repeat rows at top of page** option.

1 Display the **Page Setup** dialog box.

2 Select the **Sheet** tab.

3 Click in the **Print Titles** area, in the **Rows to repeat at top** field and enter the range, e.g. 1:3.

Or

◆ Drag over the range required.

4 Click **OK**.

Headers and footers

Headers and footers display information at the top or bottom of every printed page. They are useful for page numbers, your name, the date of printing, the worksheet name, the workbook name – or any other information that you would like to appear in them.

To add a header and/or footer to your pages:

1 Open the **Page Setup** dialog box.

2 Select the **Header/Footer** tab.

3 Choose a header or footer from the list of options available.

4 Click **OK**.

Gridlines, row and column headings

When you print your worksheet out, the gridlines, row and column headings do not print. This is usually how you would want it, but there may be times when it is useful to print them out – for example, when printing out the formulas.

To show gridlines and headings:

1 Display the **Page Setup** and select the **Sheet** tab.

2 In the **Print** options, select the **Gridlines** and/or **Row and column headings** checkboxes as required.

3 Click **OK**.

Print

When you are happy with the preview, you can send it to print.

1 Click **Print...** on the Print Preview toolbar.

Or

◆ Click the **Print** button on the Standard toolbar.

2 Complete the **Print** dialog box as required – specify the **Print range, Copies** and **Print what** options as required.

3 Click **OK**.

You can print part of a worksheet, if that is all that is required.

To print part of your worksheet:

1 Select the range of cells you want to print.

2 Open the **File** menu and choose **Print...**

3 Choose **Selection** from the **Print what** options.

4 Click **OK**.

5.19 Charts

Excel can create charts – bar graphs, line graphs, pie charts, scatter diagrams, etc. – from the data in your worksheet.

You can create your chart as an object on the same worksheet as the data on which the chart is built, or you can create the chart on a separate chart sheet.

♦ Data that you want to chart should *ideally* be in cells that are adjacent to each other. If the data has blank rows or columns within it, remove these before you try to chart the data.

To chart data that is not in adjacent cells:

1 Select the first range of cells you want to chart.

2 Hold down [**Ctrl**] while you click and drag over the other ranges you want to include in your chart.

♦ When the non-adjacent cells are selected, the selected areas *must* be able to combine to form a rectangle.

	A	B	C	D	E	F	G
1		**BOOKSHOP SALE**					
2							
3	Title	Rec Retail Price	Sale Price	Saving	No in Stock	Value of Stock	
4	Cats	£ 12.00	£ 4.80	£ 7.20	4	£ 19.20	
5	Wine tasting holidays	£ 14.00	£ 5.60	£ 8.40	6	£ 33.60	
6	Canal boat holidays	£ 10.00	£ 4.00	£ 6.00	12	£ 48.00	
7	Italian Family Cookbook	£ 14.50	£ 5.80	£ 8.70	8	£ 46.40	
8							
9						£ 147.20	
10							

Chart Wizard

The Chart Wizard will step you through the process of setting up your chart.

To create a chart:

1 Select the data to chart – including the column and row headings.

2 Click the **Chart Wizard** tool 🏭 on the Standard toolbar.

3 At step 1 of the Chart Wizard, select the **Chart type**.

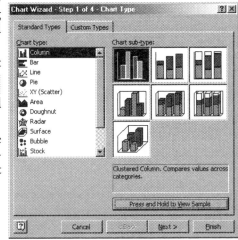

- Click the **Press and Hold to View Sample** button to see what your data would look like in your chosen chart type.

4 Once you've decided on a type, click **Next**.

5 At step 2, on the **Data Range** tab, check the data range, decide whether you want to display the data series in rows or columns (try both and decide which you prefer). Click **Next**.

6 At step 3, explore the **Chart Options** dialog box and select the options. You can add a chart or axes titles here (**Titles** tab), or reposition the Legend (**Legend** tab). Click **Next** to move on.

7 Finally, decide where the chart should be located – in your worksheet, or on a separate chart sheet and click **Finish**.

- Once a chart has been created, changes made to the data on which the chart is based, will automatically be reflected in the chart. This happens regardless of whether the chart is an object in your worksheet, or on a separate Chart Sheet.

A chart in your worksheet

The Chart toolbar should be displayed when the chart in your worksheet is selected.

Format

Chart object

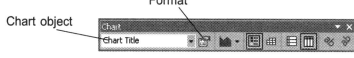

- If the chart is selected, there will be *handles* in each corner and along each side.

- If you click on the worksheet area, the chart is de-selected, and the Chart toolbar disappears.

- To select the chart again, click on it once.

Move, resize and delete chart

If you want to move, resize or delete a chart you must first select the *chart area* – either point to the chart area within the chart and click (a prompt will tell you what the mouse is pointing at) or choose **Chart Area** from the chart object list on the Chart toolbar.

To move the chart:

1 Select the chart area.

2 Drag the chart to its new position.

To resize the chart:

1 Select the chart.

2 Drag on a handle at the edge of the chart to adjust its size.

To delete the chart:

1 Select the chart.

2 Press [**Delete**].

A chart on a separate sheet

If you opt to locate your chart in a new sheet, it will be displayed on a sheet called *Chart1* (or *Chart2* or *Chart3* for later charts). The Chart sheet is inserted to the left of the sheet holding its data.

The Chart toolbar should be displayed when the Chart sheet is selected. You can use the Chart toolbar, or the **Format** or **Chart** menu to modify the chart as required.

You can change the Chart1 sheet name to something more meaningful, move the sheet to another location in your workbook, or delete the chart sheet if you decide you don't need it any more.

Chart menu

The **Chart** menu appears when you have a chart selected. Take a look at its options and their dialog boxes:

◆ **Chart Type...** displays the dialog box from Step 1 of the Wizard. You access all the chart types and sub-types from here.

◆ **Source Data...** displays the dialog box from Step 2 of the Wizard. Use this to edit the data range.

◆ **Chart Options...** displays the dialog box from Step 3 of the Wizard. You can add titles, edit the legend, gridlines, etc. here.

◆ **Location...** displays the dialog box from Step 4 of the Wizard. You can change the location of the selected chart from here – move it to another sheet, or put it on a Chart sheet.

Chart objects

Each area of your chart is an object – you have a chart area object, plot area object, category axis object, legend object, etc.

The chart must be selected (if it is an object in your workbook) before you can select the individual objects within it.

To select a chart object:

• Choose the object required from the **Chart Objects** list.

Or

• Click on the object you want to select.

Formatting chart objects

You can change the formatting of each object in your chart, e.g. the colours of the bars in a bar chart, or the position of the legend.

To format an object in your chart:

• Select the object, e.g. the legend, a data series, the title.

• Use the italic, bold, underline, font, font size, fill, text colour, etc. tools on the Formatting toolbar.

Or

• Double-click the chart object to open its Format dialog box. Explore these boxes to see and experiment with the various Formatting options for different objects.

To change the chart type

If your chart doesn't look the way you expected, and you think a different chart type would be better, you can change the chart type at any time.

To change the chart type:

1 Click the drop-down arrow by the **Chart Type** tool on the Chart toolbar.

2 Select the type of chart required.

Printing charts

You can print a chart with or without the data on which it is based. To print a chart that is an object within your worksheet you have several options. I suggest you do a Print Preview before you actually print, just to check it looks okay.

To print out all of the data on the worksheet *and* the chart:

1 Print the worksheet as normal (with the chart de-selected).

To get a printout of the chart only:

1 Select the chart on the worksheet, then print.

To get the chart, and its data only:

1 Select the chart.

2 Click the **Data Table** tool 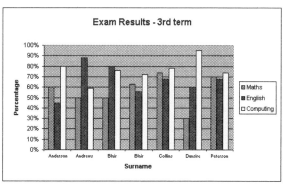 on the Chart toolbar to display the data table for the chart.

3 Print out with the chart selected.

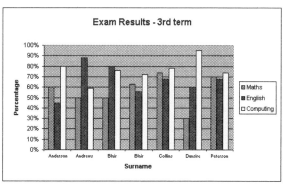

To print a chart that is on a separate chart sheet:

1 Select the chart sheet.

2 Print as usual.

* If you also want to print out the data on which the chart is based, display the data table before you print.

You can use the drawing tools to create different effects on your worksheet data and charts. If you create charts, try using an arrow and a text box to add emphasis to it (see section 3.11).

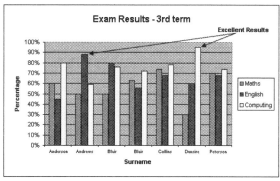

Summary

In this chapter you have learnt about:

- Worksheets and workbooks
- Moving around your worksheet
- Selection techniques
- Entering text and data into a worksheet
- Adjusting column widths and row heights
- Fitting text into cells
- Formatting options that are specific to spreadsheets
- Freeze headings and split screen
- Entering formulas using the operators
- AutoSum and AutoFill
- Statistical functions – Average, Minimum, Maximum, Count
- Viewing formulas
- Sorting your data
- The IF function
- Absolute addressing
- Page Setup and Print
- Creating and manipulating charts

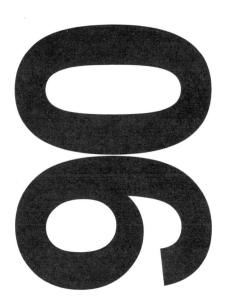

06

databases

In this chapter you will learn

- about Access and databases
- how to create tables
- how to enter and edit data
- how to extract records
- how to produce reports

6.1 Planning and design

A simple database could be used to store names and addresses (e.g. your Christmas card list), or details of your CD collection, or a more complex one could organize the data you need to run your company (supplier, customer, stock, order details, etc.).

In a simple database, it may be feasible to store all the information together in one table – as you could with a Christmas card list. Other databases are more complex with several tables, e.g. a company database with details of customers, staff and suppliers.

Some database terminology may be unfamiliar to you. Below are brief definitions of the terms you are likely to encounter.

Term	Definition
Table	All the data on one topic is stored in a table. In a simple database, you might have only one table. More complex ones may consist of several tables.
Record	The data for a single item in your table, e.g. the details relating to one book in a Library table.
Field	A piece of data within a record, e.g. in a book's record, things like ISBN, title or author.
Relationship	Links the detail in one table to the detail in another, e.g. through the ISBN.
Join	The process of linking tables or queries.
Data definition	The process of defining what data will be stored, specifying the field's type (number, text, etc.), size and how it is related to data in other tables.
Data manipulation	Work done on an existing database, e.g. sorting it into an order, extracting records from tables, or listing detail from several tables in one report.

Example database

In this chapter we will set up a database that could be used to record details of the books in a library. It will hold these details:

♦ Book title, author, price, year published.

♦ Publisher name, address and other contact details.

Schematic diagram of a database

LIBRARY DATABASE

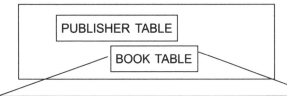

BOOK TABLE

ISBN	Title	First Name	Last Name	Price	Year	Publisher Code
0-123-12345-1	The Planets	Joe	Simpson	£15.00	1999	1001
0-321-54321-1	Outdoor Cooking	Angela	Armstrong	£7.50	2003	1025
0-111-22222-3	The Kitchen Garden	Brian	Wilson	£22.00	1975	1100
0-222-11111-3	Corvette	Karen	Andrews	£10.50	1985	1250

The diagram illustrates our database.

♦ Each *record* in a table is presented in a *row*.

♦ Each *field* in a record is in a *column*.

♦ Each field has a *field name* at the top of the column.

Access objects

An Access database consists of *objects* that can be used to input, display, interrogate, print and automate your work. These objects are listed in the Database window. The ones we will be using are:

♦ **Tables** – the most important objects in your database. Tables hold your data and are used for data entry and editing. They display data in a datasheet (it looks like an Excel worksheet).

♦ **Queries** – used to locate specific records in your tables using various criteria, e.g. overdue books, or all science fiction books.

♦ **Forms** – used to provide an alternative and more 'user friendly' front end to your tables for entering and editing records.

♦ **Reports** – used to produce various printed outputs from the data in your database.

Preparing your data

Before you set up a database you should work out the answers to a couple of questions:

- What data do you want to store in the database? (e.g. authors' names, book titles, etc.)

- What information do you want to get out of your database? (e.g. a list of all books that are overdue, a list of all books by a particular author, etc.)

If you work out the answers to these questions, you will be in a position to start working out what fields you need.

If you are setting up names, you would probably break the name into three fields – Title, First name (or Initials) and Last name. This way you can sort the file into Last name order, or search for someone using the First name and Last name.

If you are storing addresses, you would probably want separate fields for Street, Town/City, Region, PostCode and/or Country. You can then sort your records into order on any of these fields, or locate records by specifying search criteria. For example, using Street and Town/City fields, you could search for details of people who live in St John's Street, Stirling rather than St John's Street, Dundee.

When planning your database, take a small sample of the data you wish to store and examine it carefully. This will help you confirm what fields will be required.

You must also decide how much space is required for each field. The space you allocate must be long enough to accommodate the longest item that might go there. How long is the longest last name you want to store? If in doubt, take a sample of some typical names (Anderson, Johnston, Mackenzie, Harvey-Jones) and add a few more characters to the longest one to be sure.

Primary Key

Most records will have a unique identifier – a field that holds different information in every record. In our database, each book would have an ISBN number and this would be different (unique) for each book. The field that must be unique in each record is set as the Primary Key. You cannot enter duplicate information into a primary key field – Access will not allow it.

Try to group your fields into tables with a view to minimizing the duplication of data in your database.

There are several benefits to this approach:

• Each set of details is stored (and therefore keyed in) only once.

• The tables are smaller than they otherwise might have been.

• As you don't have much duplication of data, the database is easier to maintain and keep up to date.

It is very important that you spend time organizing and structuring your data before you start to computerize it – it'll save you a lot of time and frustration in the long run!

6.2 Starting Access

When you start Access, the Access screen will appear with the New File task pane on the right.

To create our Library database:

• Click **Blank Database** on the New file Task Pane.

Or

If you are already in Access, but have not yet created the Library database file, do so now:

• Click the **New** tool on the **Database** toolbar, then click Blank Database on the New file Task Pane.

You arrive at the **File New Database** dialog box.

Where do you want to store your database? *My Documents* is the default – select the folder or drive in the **Save in** field.

As with all Microsoft packages, a temporary filename is suggested – in Access these follow the pattern *db1, db2, db3*. You need to replace the temporary name with one that means something to you, and reflects the contents of your database.

The example database used here is one that may help in the running of a library. Name your database *Library*.

• Once you have named your database click the **Create** button.

This takes you through into Access, with your Library database window displayed.

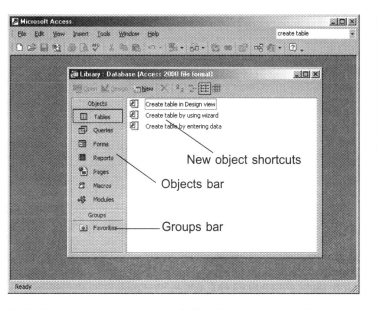

New object shortcuts

Objects bar

Groups bar

6.3 Data types and field properties

Data types

There are 10 different data types to choose from when setting up your table structures. Most of your fields will probably be Text, with a few of the others used in each table depending on the type of data you wish to store. The data types that you will use most often are described here.

Data type	Usage	Size	Notes
Text	Alphanumeric data	up to 255 bytes	Default data type
Number	Numeric data	1,2,4 or 8 bytes	
Date/Time	Dates and times	8 bytes	Values for the years 100 through to 9999
Currency	Monetary data	8 bytes	Accurate to 4 decimal places and 15 digits to the left of the decimal separator
AutoNumber	Unique long integer created by Access	4 bytes	Cannot be updated Useful for primary keys
Yes/No	Boolean data	1 bit	Yes and No values, and fields that contain 1 of 2 values On/Off, True/False

Properties

You can customize each field by specifying different properties. The properties vary depending on the data type. The properties most commonly used are listed here.

Property	Data type	Notes
Field Size	Text and Number	Text from 1 to 255 characters
	Number field sizes are: • Byte (single byte) • Integer (2-byte) • Long Integer (4-byte) • Single (4-byte) • Double (8-byte)	Values: • 0 to 255 • -32,768 to +32,767 • -2,147,483,647 to 2,147,483,647 • -3.4×10^{38} to 3.4×10^{38} • -1.797×10^{308} to $+1.797 \times 10^{308}$
Format		Options depend on the data type
Decimal places	Number and Currency	Auto (displays 2 d.p. for most formats) or Fixed: 0 to 15 d.p.
Caption		For display on forms and reports
Default Value	All except Memo, OLE Object and AutoNumber	
Validation Rule		Used to test that suitable data is entered
Validation Text		The message to appear on screen when a validation rule is not met
Required		Set to Yes if data must be entered
Indexed	Text, Number, Currency, Date/Time and AutoNumber types	Indexing speeds up access to its data – fields that will be sorted or queried on should be indexed

6.4 Creating a new table

* Double-click [icon] Create table in Design view.

Or

1 Select **Tables** on the Objects bar.

2 Click **New** [New] on the Database window toolbar.

3 Select **Design View**.

4 Click **OK**.

In Design view you can specify the field names, data types and any other properties you think would be useful.

Define fields in
the upper pane
…

…and
properties in
the lower pane

In the table design you identify the fields required, their data types
and any other properties that are important. We will set up two
table designs: the *Books* table and *Publisher* table.

Defining the table structure

The *Books* table will contain the fields listed below.

Field name	Data type	Properties
ISBN	Text	Primary Key, Field Size = 25
Title	Text	Field Size = 35, Indexed (Duplicates OK)
Classification	Text	Field Size = 20, Default Value = Fiction, Indexed (Duplicates OK)
Year published	Text	Field Size = 4
Publisher ID	Text	Field Size = 6
Author Firstname	Text	Field Size = 15
Author Surname	Text	Field Size = 20
Cover	Text	Field Size = 12, Default Value = Paperback
Price	Currency	Validation Rule <100 (No books in our library cost over £100)

• The Publisher ID field will be used to link to the *Publisher* table, where the contact details of each publisher will be held. This means that if we have several books from one publisher, we can store the contact details *once* in the publisher table – reducing duplication of data.

Our first field is the ISBN.

1 In the Field name column, key in the field name – 'ISBN'.

2 Press [**Tab**] to move along to the Data type column and set this to *Text* (the default data type).

• The default size for a Text field is 50 characters. This is more than is required for an ISBN, and it could be reduced to 10.

3 Press [**F6**] to move to the lower pane (or click with the mouse) and change the field size from 50 to 25, then press [**F6**] to return to the upper pane.

4 Press [**Tab**] to move along to the Description column and enter a field description if you wish.

• The Description is optional – anything typed here will appear on the Status bar (as a prompt to the operator) during data entry to that field.

The ISBN field is the primary key for this table – each book has a unique code – its unique identifier.

To establish Primary Key status, click the **Primary Key** tool when the insertion point is in the ISBN field in the upper pane.

Note that the Index property is automatically set to YES (No Duplicates) when a field is given Primary Key status.

Enter the Title details in the 2nd row of the upper pane.

1 In the Field name column, key in the field name – Title.

2 Press [**Tab**] to move to the Data type column and set this to Text.

3 Set the field size to 35.

4 Set the Indexed property to *Yes (Duplicates OK)*.

Enter the remaining fields following the suggestions in the table.

1 Click the **Save** tool on the Table Design toolbar.

2 Give your table a suitable name e.g. *Books*.

3   Click **OK**.

4   Close the Table Design window.

The table will be listed under Tables in the **Database** window.

Setting up the Publisher table

1   Create a new table as above, but with the information given below.

2   Set up the structure for this table, following the suggestions.

3   Save and close the table.

Field name	Data type	Properties	Notes
Publisher ID	Text	Field Size = 6	Primary Key
Company Name	Text	Field Size = 35	Indexed (Duplicates OK)
Address	Text	Field Size = 30	
Town	Text	Field Size = 20	Indexed (Duplicates OK), Default Value = London
Postcode	Text	Field Size = 10	
Telephone No	Text	Field Size = 20	
Email	Text	Field Size = 40	

♦   Save the table and close the Table Design window.

Primary Key/Foreign Key

A Primary Key field is the one that is the unique identifier in each table. In the tables above, the Primary Key in the *Books* table is the ISBN, and in the *Publisher* table it is the Publisher ID.

The Publisher ID appears in the Books table. Although an ID field, it is not the primary key in this table – it is a Foreign Key. A Foreign Key refers to a Primary Key in another table.

6.5 Relationships

We now have to set up the relationships between these tables.

1   Click the **Relationships** tool 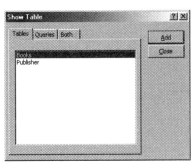 on the Database toolbar at the Database window. The Relationships window opens.

♦   The **Show Table** window should also be displayed – if it isn't, click the **Show Table** tool to display a list of the tables.

2   Select the table(s) to add to the **Relationships** window and click **Add**.

3   Click **Close** once you have added your tables.

We need to create a relationship:

♦   Between the *Books* and *Publisher* table using the Publisher ID.

With the tables related, we will be able to pull information from more than one table at a time if necessary.

Relationship types

One-to-many – one of the related fields is a Primary Key or has a unique index. This is the most common type of relationship. In our example a Publisher in the *Publisher* table can have many matching records in the *Books* table – a one-to-many relationship.

One-to-one – both the related fields are Primary Keys or contain unique indexes. Each record in the first table can have only one matching record in the second, and vice versa. One-to-one relationships are sometimes used to divide a table that has many fields, or to isolate fields for security reasons. This type of relationship may be used when storing personnel data where you could have general information in one table, e.g. name, address, job title, and confidential information in another, e.g. salary, bank details, etc.

Referential integrity

These are the rules that are followed to preserve the defined relationships between tables when you enter or delete records.

If you enforce *referential integrity*, Access prevents you from:

- Adding records to a related table when there is no associated record in the primary table.

- Changing a value in the primary table that would result in unconnected records in a related table.

- Deleting records from the primary table when there are matching related records in a related table.

To create a relationship:

1 Click on the field you wish to relate to another table.

2 Drag the field and drop it onto the field you wish to link it to in the other table.

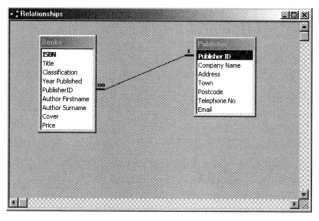

3 At the **Edit Relationships** dialog box, select **Referential Integrity** (if desired) and click **Create** to establish the relationship.

4 Click **OK**.

The lines running between the fields linking the tables are called *join lines*.

To delete an existing relationship:

1 Click on the Join Line you wish to remove to select it.

2 Press [**Delete**].

3 Respond to the prompt as required.

- Save the changes made to the **Relationship** window if you wish to keep them and close the window when you have done.

6.6 Entering data in Datasheet view

You should have the Library database open. The two tables will be listed in the **Tables** area of the Database window.

Data entry is generally easy. You simply open the table and key in the data – using [Tab] or the mouse to move from field to field. As you are keying in the data, look out for these features.

*   To open a table in Datasheet view, double-click on its name, or select the table required in the **Tables** list and click **Open**.

In Datasheet view, your table looks similar to a spreadsheet layout – each record is presented in a row and each field is in a column.

*   To move forward through the fields press [**Tab**].

*   To move backward through the fields press [**Shift**]-[**Tab**].

*   Or click in the field you want to move to using the mouse.

For the *Publisher* table, enter the records shown on page 171.

You will notice that the Town field is completed automatically with London – our default value. Make up another 6 records.

*   Close the table when you've finished entering your data (you don't need to save your data, Access does this automatically).

For the *Books* table, enter details of the books that you have in your library, or use the data on page 171. Add another 10, using the same classifications.

*   Close the table when you've finished.

Editing data in Datasheet view

At the bottom left of the table window, you will find a set of navigation buttons that you can use to move through your table in Datasheet view, instead of using [**Tab**] or the mouse.

The record number field tells you the current record, beside it you will find the total number of records in your table.

If you spot an error in Datasheet view, you must position the insertion point within the field before you can edit it.

Publisher Table

Pub ID	Company Name	Address	Town	Postcode	Telephone No	Email
P1	Hodder & Stoughton	338 Euston Road	London	NW1 3BH	02071 111 2222	hodinfo@hotmail.com
P2	Westward Lock Ltd	18 Clifftop Street	London	WIX 1RB		Gill.A@yahoo.com
P3	Alice Publications	4 High Street	Oxford	OX1 2QQ		a.smith@hotmail.com
P4	Puffin Books	3 West Row	London	NW2 3SL	02081 222 3333	

Books Table

ISBN	Title	Classification	Year pub'd	PublisherID	Author Firstname	Author Secondname	Cover	Price
01-12345-123	The Snow Storm	Fiction	1985	P2	Gill	Peterson	Paperback	£7.99
02-54321-321	Indian Highlights	Travel	1997	P3	Andrew	Borthwick	Paperback	£9.99
03-13243-312	Elm Grove	Children's	1996	P2	Clare	Adams	Paperback	£6.99
04-53423-222	Africa Trekker	Travel	1994	P1	Andrew	Borthwick	Paperback	£6.99
05-11111-222	The Lying Stone	Fiction	1954	P4	Kim	Simpson	Hardback	£16.99

You can use the scroll bars (horizontal and vertical), or the navigation buttons to locate the record. You can then click in the field and insert or delete data as necessary.

If you use [**Tab**] or [**Shift**]-[**Tab**] techniques to move through the fields, the contents of a field are selected when you move on to it.

- To replace the selected data within a field, simply key in the new text – whatever you key in will replace the original data.

- To delete the data, press [**Delete**] when it is still selected.

- To add or delete data without removing the current contents of the field, deselect the field contents before you edit. Click into the field, or press [F2]. Once the data is deselected you can position the insertion point and insert or delete as required.

To add a record:

1   Click the **New Record** tool on the Table Datasheet toolbar.

2   Enter your record details into the empty row.

To delete a record:

1   Place the insertion point within the record you wish to delete.

2   Click the **Delete Record** tool on the Table Datasheet toolbar.

6.7 Formatting in Datasheet view

If you don't like the formatting on your datasheet you can try something else. The Font, Datasheet, Row Height and Column Width options described below are applied to the whole table – you don't need to select anything first.

To set the font:

1   Choose **Font…** from the **Format** menu.

2   Select the font style, size and attributes required.

3   Click **OK**.

To set the Datasheet options:

1   Choose **Datasheet…** from the **Format** menu.

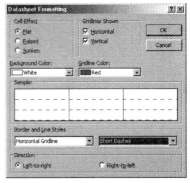

2 Specify the **Cell Effect, Background Color**, which **Gridlines** to show, the **Gridline Color** and the **Border and Line styles**.

3 Click **OK**.

To set the row height:

1 Choose **Row Height…** from the **Format** menu.

2 Specify a row height, or select the **Standard Height** checkbox.

3 Click **OK**.

To set the column width:

1 Place the insertion point anywhere within the column.

2 Choose **Column Width…** from the **Format** menu.

3 Specify the width required or select **Standard Width** and click **OK**.

Or

• Let Access work out the best size by choosing *Best Fit.*

6.8 Changing the table structure

To edit the table structure you must take your table into Design view. You can do this from the Database window if you select the table you need to edit on the **Tables** tab, and click **Design**.

Alternatively, if you are already in Datasheet view, you can go into Design view by clicking the **View** tool [icon].

• To move back into Datasheet view afterwards, click the **View** tool [icon] on the Table Design toolbar.

To add a new field at the end of the table:

• Scroll down until you reach the empty row under the existing fields. Enter the field name, data type and properties.

To add a new field between two existing fields:

1 Place the insertion point in the upper pane anywhere within the field that will be below your new field.

2 Click the **Insert Rows** tool [icon] – a new row is inserted above the one the insertion point is in.

3 Enter the field name, data type, etc. as required.

To delete a field:

1 Place the insertion point in the upper pane within the field.

2 Click the **Delete Rows** tool ⬚.

3 Respond to the prompt – choose Yes to delete the field, No if you've changed your mind.

Be careful when you delete fields – any data held within that field in your records will be lost.

To change the field properties:

1 Place the insertion point in the upper pane within the field.

2 Press [**F6**] to move to the lower pane.

3 Edit the properties as required.

4 Press [**F6**] to return to the upper pane.

When changing a field size, watch that you don't end up losing data. If you reduce the size, any record that has data in that field in excess of the new size will have the extra characters cut off!

To change the field that has Primary Key status:

1 Place the insertion point within the field in the upper pane that you want to take Primary Key status.

2 Click the **Primary Key** tool.

To remove Primary Key status, and not give it to any other field:

1 Place the insertion point within the field in the upper pane that currently has Primary Key status.

2 Click the **Primary Key** tool ⬚.

To rename a field:

♦ Edit the name you wish to change in the first column in the upper pane.

To move a field:

1 Click in the row selector bar to the left of the field.

2 Drag and drop the field into its new position – a thick dark horizontal line that indicates where the field will move to.

To keep the fields in their new position you must save the design before you close your table.

When you close your table, you will be asked if you wish to save the layout changes. Respond **Yes** (to save), **No** (to close the table without saving) or **Cancel** (to return to the table to do more work).

6.9 AutoForm

As an alternative to entering data into a table in Datasheet view, you could use Form view.

In Datasheet view, each record is displayed in a row, each field in a column. As many fields and records are displayed in the table window as will fit.

In Form view, the fields are arranged attractively on the screen (you can design forms to resemble paper forms you actually use) and one record is displayed at a time. Form view is often considered more 'user friendly' than Datasheet view.

Access has a useful tool that builds a simple form automatically – AutoForm.

• Try it out by creating forms for your *Books* table and *Publisher* table.

To create an AutoForm for a table:

1 Select the table you wish to use from the Tables list in the Database window, e.g. *Books*.

2 On the Database toolbar, click the drop-down arrow to the right of the **New Object** tool.

3 Choose **AutoForm**.

The table you selected is displayed using a simple form layout (*Books* table), or form with a subform (*Publisher* table).

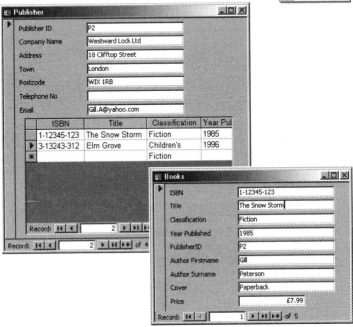

You can move around in Form view in the same way as you did in Datasheet view:

- Press [**Tab**] or [**Shift**]-[**Tab**] to move from field to field, or click in the field you want to input or edit.
- Use the navigation buttons to move from record to record, or to the first or last record in the table.
- To go to a specific record number, click into the record number field, type the number you wish to go to and press [**Enter**].
- Click the new record button to get a blank form.
- Use the scroll bars to move around a large form.

The data you enter or edit in your form in Form view will be stored in the table on which the form is based. Even if you opt not to save the form itself, the data will still be stored in the table.

If you have been working on your table in Datasheet view, you can easily change to Form view using the **AutoForm** tool.

Changing Views

When working with a form, you have three views that you should be familiar with – Design, Datasheet and Form.

To change views:

1 Click the drop-down arrow to the right of the **View** tool.

2 Click on the view required.

- Design View
- Form View
- Datasheet View
- PivotTable View
- PivotChart View

6.10 Form Design

The actual *design* of a form can be viewed and adjusted in Form Design view.

To take your form into Design view:

- Choose **Design View** from the **View** options.

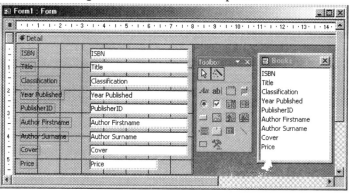

The Form Design window will appear on your screen.

The Form is designed on a grid.

The Field List (displaying the field names from the table on which you are building the form) and the Toolbox (used to add labels, lines, etc. to your form) may also be displayed.

- Click the **Field List** tool ▦ to toggle the display of the Field List.

- Click the **Toolbox** tool ▓ to toggle the display of the Toolbox.

The main areas in a form:

- Detail Area
- Form Header and Footer area
- Page Header and Footer area

The **Detail** area is present on every form. It is the part of your form in which most of the detail from your table will be displayed.

The **Form Header and Footer** areas appear above and below the Detail area for each record in Form view. Form Headers and Footers are optional and can be used for titles or instructions you wish to appear above and below each form.

To toggle the Form Headers and Footers on and off:

1 Open the **View** menu.

2 Choose **Form Header/Footer**.

The **Page Headers and Footers** appear at the top and bottom of each page, should you opt to print your form out.

To toggle the Page Headers and Footers on and off:

1 Open the **View** menu.

2 Choose **Page Header/Footer**.

If you enter any data into the Form or Page Header or Footer area, then opt *not* to display the area, the data you entered will be lost.

The form above could be modified by adding a heading (in the Form Header area) containing the text 'Library Book Details'. The text 'Library Book Details' would be placed in a *label*.

Labels are used for instructions or headings – in fact any text that doesn't come from the underlying table.

Text

To add text:

1 Display the Form Header and Footer areas.

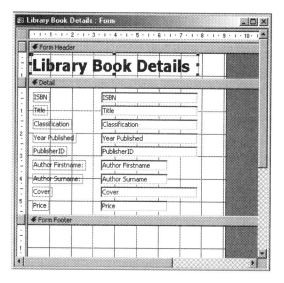

2   Click the **Label** tool 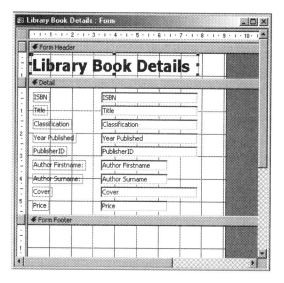 in the Toolbox.

3   Move the pointer into the Form Header area (notice the pointer shape is now +A).

4   Click in the Form Header area where you want the heading to go.

5   Key in your heading.

6   Click anywhere outside the label field.

♦   To resize the Form Header or Footer area drag the bottom edge of it (the pointer will change to a double-headed arrow when you are in the correct place).

The objects (fields, labels, etc.) on your form can be moved, resized, formatted or deleted – so it's not critical that you get everything right first time.

To edit an object: click on it to select it. You will notice that a selected field has handles around it – one in each corner and one halfway along each side.

To resize: click and drag a handle in the direction required.

To move a field: point to its edge (not over a handle) and drag – the pointer looks like a hand when you are in the right place.

To delete a field: press [Delete].

To change the formatting: use the tools on the Formatting (Form/Report) toolbar.

- You could format the heading that you put on your *Books* form. If you increase the size of the font, you may need to increase the size of the label so that all of the text is displayed.

- To make your form wider, drag its right-most edge.

Pictures

To add a picture to your form:

1 Display and/or resize the area where you want the picture, e.g. Form Header area, or Form Footer area or Detail area.

2 Select the **Image** tool ▦ in the Toolbox.

3 Click in the area that you want the picture to appear.

- The **Insert Picture** dialog box will appear.

4 Locate and select the picture – double-click on it.

5 You will be returned to your form.

6 Resize/move your picture as necessary.

Experiment with the picture size mode to see the various effects.

1 Double-click on the picture to open its Properties dialog box.

2 Locate the **Size Mode** field (on the third field on the **Format** tab or fourth field on the **All** tab).

3 Select *Clip*, *Stretch* or *Zoom* as required.

4 Close the dialog box – click **Close**.

If you do not like the Size Mode effect, repeat steps 1–4 and select a different one.

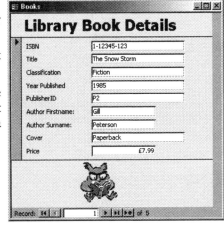

Background colour

To change the background colour of your form:

1 Select the area to format – Detail, Header, Footer, etc.

2 Click the drop-down arrow beside the **Fill/Back Color** tool 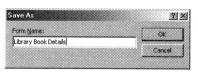.

3 Choose a colour.

♦ Choose **Form View** from the View options to display your results.

Saving your form

To save your form, click the **Save** tool on the Form Design toolbar. At the **Save As** dialog box, accept the default name, or edit it, then click **OK**.

If you close your form without first saving it, Access will ask you if you want to save the form.

♦ **Yes** will take you to the Save As dialog box.

♦ **No** will close the form without saving it.

♦ **Cancel** will return you to Form view.

If you save your form, it will be listed under Forms in the Database window. You can open the form again from this list at any time – either double-click on the form name or select the form name and click **Open**.

6.11 Form Wizard

You can also create a form using the Form Wizard. Use this where the fields are taken from more than one table, and when you want to use a preset colour scheme/design.

1 Select **Forms** in the Objects bar.

2 Double-click Create form by using wizard .

3 Select the table or query you wish to use a field from.

4 Select the field and click to add it to the *selected fields* list.

5 Repeat steps 3–4 until all fields have been added, then click **Next**.

6 If you have selected fields from more than one table or query, you will be asked how you want to view the form – experiment with the options and then select one.

7 Choose the layout required and click **Next**.

8 Select a style, and then click **Next**.

9 Amend the suggested Form name(s) if you wish.

10 Select *Open the form to view or edit information.*

11 Click **Finish**.

♦ Experiment with the wizard – you can create some useful forms very easily this way. If you wish to 'tweak' the form, take it into Design view and work on it there.

6.12 Printing your tables

You can print the contents of your tables from Datasheet view or from the Database window (simply select the table you want to print before you click the **Print** tool). See section 3.4 for details on Preview and Print.

Margins and orientation

If you need to change the margins or the orientation of your table before you print it, you must go into the **Page Setup** options.

1 Open your table in Datasheet view.

2 Select **Page Setup…** from the **File** menu.

♦ On the **Margins** tab of the dialog box, you can change the top, bottom, left or right margins. You can also specify whether or not you want to print the field name (**Print headings** option) at the top of each field.

♦ On the **Page** tab, you can change the orientation (portrait or landscape), the paper size and source details, and the printer details.

6.13 Sort

You can easily sort a table into ascending or descending order based on the data in one field.

1 Open the table you are going to sort.

2 Place the insertion point anywhere within the field you want to sort the records on.

3 Click the **Sort Ascending** [icon] or **Sort Descending** [icon] tool.

When you close a table that you have sorted, you will be asked if you want to save the changes. To save the records in the new, sorted order, choose **Yes**, otherwise, choose **No**.

Multi-level sort

If you want to sort your table on several fields, you must set up your sort requirements in the **Filter** dialog box.

You could sort your *Books* Table into ascending order on Classification, and then by Title. Open your *Books* Table to try this out.

1 Open the **Records** menu, point to **Filter** and select **Advanced Filter/Sort…**

• In the upper half of the **Filter** dialog box the field list of the current table is displayed. Scroll through the list until you see the field you want to use for your main sort.

2 Double-click on the field name – it will appear in the first row, first column of the query grid.

3 Select the options in the **Sort** row below the field name.

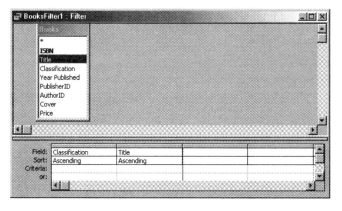

4   Return to the upper pane and double-click on the field for your second-level sort, then set its sort order.

5   Click the **Apply Filter** tool 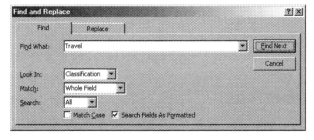 on the Filter/Sort toolbar to display your records in the new order.

You can save the options you have set up as a Query. You must return to the **Filter** dialog box to do this (use **Records** > **Filter** > **Advanced Filter/Sort…**).

1   Click the **Save As Query** tool on the Filter/Sort toolbar.

2   Give your query a suitable name.

3   Click **OK**.

Your query will be listed under Queries in the Database window.

6.14 Find

To locate a record in your table, you can use the navigation buttons, or go to a record by specifying its number in the number field in the navigation buttons and pressing [**Enter**]. You can also locate records using **Find**.

1   In Datasheet view, place the insertion point within the field that contains the text you want to find.

2   Click the **Find** tool on the Table Datasheet toolbar.

3   Type what you are looking for in the **Find What** field.

4   Edit the other fields as necessary.

5   Click **Find Next** to find the first matching record.

6   If it is not the record you want, click **Find Next** until you reach the correct record.

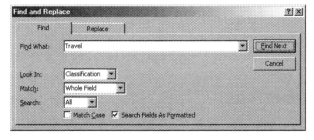

7   Close the dialog box once you have found your record.

If Access can't find what you are looking for, a dialog box will appear telling you that the search string wasn't found. If this happens, check your entry in the **Find What** fields carefully – you may have typed it incorrectly.

6.15 Filter

If you want to display a specific group of records, this can be done by filtering them. You can filter 'By Selection' or 'By Form'.

Filter By Selection

1   Open the table in Datasheet view if necessary.

2   Position the insertion point in the field of a record that has the criterion you are looking for.

3   Click the **Filter By Selection** tool .

A subset of the records within your table will be displayed.

* You can filter your filtered list again using the same technique – narrowing down your list of records as you go.

* To display all your records, click the **Remove Filter** tool .

Filter By Form

When you Filter By Form, you can specify multiple criteria (unlike Filter By Selection where you narrow down your search one criterion at a time). You can also use operators in your search.

Operators

If you want to specify a range of values you must use these operators in your expressions:

=	Equal to	<>	Not equal to
<	Less than	>	Greater than
<=	Less than or equal to	>=	Greater than or equal to
Is Null	Empty field	Is Not Null	Field has an entry

You can also set a range using the keywords **Between...And...**

To filter by form:

1 Click the **Filter By Form** tool 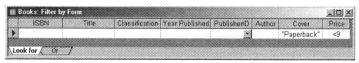.

♦ You are presented with an empty record. As you move from field to field, notice you can display a list of options for each.

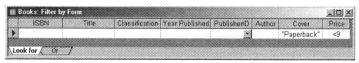

2 Select the filter criteria using the drop-down lists, and/or type in your criteria using the appropriate operators.

3 Click the **Apply Filter** tool – all records meeting the criteria specified will be displayed.

4 To display all your records again, click **Remove Filter**.

As with a multi-level sort in 6.13, you can save the options you have specified in the Filter by Form window as a Query.

1 Click the **Save As Query** tool.

2 Give your query a suitable name.

3 Click **OK**.

Your query will be listed under Queries in the Database window.

6.16 Query Design

You can sort your data, or specify criteria, in Query Design view.

Using Query Design View:

1 Select **Queries** in the Objects bar.

2 Double-click [🗐 Create query in Design view].

You will arrive at the Select Query dialog box. The Show Table window should be open, listing the tables in your database.

♦ If the Show Table window is not open, click the **Show Table** tool to display the table list.

3 Add the table(s) required to the **Select Query** dialog box – *Publisher* in this example.

4 Close the Show Table window.

You will notice some extra rows in the lower pane of the Select Query window.

* The **Table** row displays the name of the table from which a field is taken.

* The sort order is specified in the **Sort** row.

* The **Show** row indicates whether or not a selected field will be displayed in the result – a tick in the box means the field detail will be displayed, no tick means the detail will not be displayed. The default is that the detail will be displayed.

* The **Criteria** row(s) is where you tell Access the rules that you want to apply for selection.

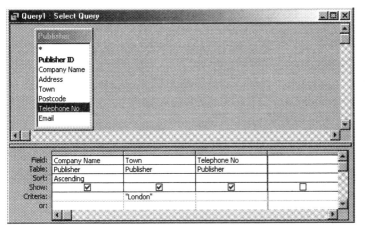

1 Select the fields you want, in the order you want them to appear – double-click on them in the field list.

2 Specify the sort order and/or criteria.

* In this example, we want publishers based in London, sorted into ascending order on Company name.

3 Run your query – click the **Run** tool 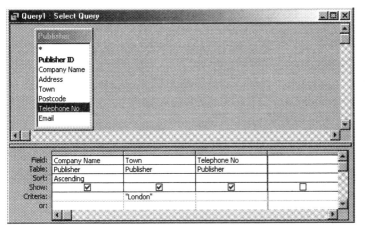 on the Query Design toolbar.

4 Save your query if you want to reuse it.

5 Close your query.

Specifying criteria

The criteria are specified through expressions that you key into the **Criteria** rows in the query grid. When entering expressions there are a couple of rules you should keep in mind.

• When you enter criteria in different cells in the same criteria row, Access uses the **And** operator. It looks for **all** the conditions being met before returning the record details.

• If you enter criteria in different cells in different criteria rows, Access uses the **Or** operator.

Querying multiple tables

There may be times when you need to collect the data you require from several tables, and sort or filter that data. When working across several tables, you must set up a query in the Query Design window. In this example the query produces a list of authors' names, the title of their books, and the names of their publishers.

1 Work through steps 1–4 in Query Design above – opt to show both tables at the **Show Table** dialog box.

2 Specify the criteria and sort order.

3 Save the query.

4 Run it.

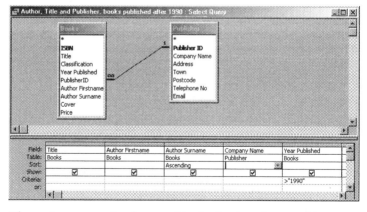

The main purpose (and strength) of a database is to enable you to store your data (maybe tens of thousands of records in a real business situation) and quickly extract or sort that data as required.

Experiment with the query and sorting facilities until you get the hang of them. See section 6.15 for details of the operators you can use.

Try these ones:

Books table

• Extract details of all Fiction written since 1985.

• Display details of Title, Classification and Price, sorted into Price order.

• Display a list of all books *except* those classified as Travel (<>Travel).

Publisher table

• Extract publisher Name, Town and Telephone No., displaying details of the publishers that you DO NOT have a telephone number for (Telephone No = "Is Null").

• Display publisher Name, Town and Email, in Town order.

Multiple table queries

• Display the publisher's name, book title and price for all the London publishers.

• Extract a list showing publisher name, author name, and book title for all books priced between £8 and £12.

6.17 AutoReport

Reports are used to display the data in your tables and queries in a layout that is usually easier to interpret than the datasheet.

You can quickly produce a report (in much the same way as you generate an AutoForm) from any table or query using the AutoReport object. It will be a simple, single column report, listing all the fields in each record of the table or query.

To create an AutoReport from a table or query:

1 Display the New Object list.

2 Select **AutoReport**.

• A simple report will be created using the data in the table or query you have open.

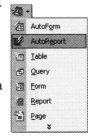

3   When you close your report you will be asked if you want to save it. If you save it, the report will be listed under Reports in the Database window.

You do not need to open a table or query before you can create an AutoReport from it – you can do so from the Database window.

To generate an AutoReport from the Database window:

1   Select the table or query you want to base your report on.

2   Choose **AutoReport** from the New Object list.

Reports are displayed in Print Preview – so you can see what your page would look like if you were to print it out.

You can use the navigation buttons at the bottom of the Print Preview window to move through the pages in your report.

◆   Click the **View** tool on the Print Preview toolbar to take your report through into Design view.

6.18 Report Wizard

You can also create a report using the Report Wizard, as you can create a form using Form Wizard (see section 6.11). This is *very* useful if you wish to group the information in your report in any way, e.g. group the books by classification. You can also perform simple summary calculations over the group, and over the whole report using the summary options.

In this example, we will display our books in a report, grouped by Classification. The books will be sorted into ascending order on Title. We will also perform a summary calculation on the Price field, to display the average price of those in each classification.

1   Select **Reports** in the Objects bar.

2   Double-click 🖼️ Create report by using wizard .

3   Select the *Books* table, and add all the fields to the *Selected Fields* list and click **Next**.

4   Specify the grouping, e.g *Classification*, and click **Next**.

5   Set the sort order, e.g. *Title*.

6   Click **Summary Options...**

7 Select **Avg** in the **Summary Options** dialog box, and select **Detail and Summary** in the **Show** options, then click **OK**.

8 Click **Next**.

9 Select a layout and specify the orientation for the page (if you have a lot of fields to display use landscape).

10 Select the **Adjust the field width so all fields fit on a page** checkbox and click **Next**.

11 Choose a **Style** and click **Next**.

12 Edit the report name if you wish, select **Preview the Report** and click **Finish**.

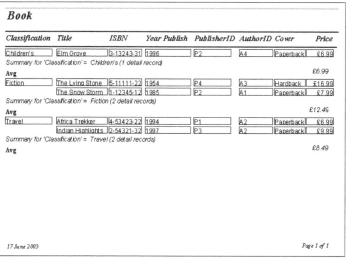

You can take the report into Design view and edit in a similar way to editing a form in Design view.

♦ Experiment with the wizard – you can design some attractive and useful reports with it quite easily.

6.19 Report Design

The Design view of a report looks very similar to the Design view of a form. You should experiment with it so that you can control the look of your reports even more.

The main areas in a report are:

- Detail area
- Page header and footer area
- Report header and footer area.

The commands to switch the Page and/or Report Header and Footer areas on and off are in the View menu.

- The page header and footer area are displayed by default in an AutoReport design.

The field list, containing the field names from the table or query on which the report is based, is displayed – you can toggle the display of this by clicking the **Field List** tool ▦.

Page header and footer

Page headers are often used for column headings, or the report title, page footers are usually used for page numbering.

You can add a page header using the **Label** tool. You used this tool in Form design to add headings and other text to your form. The same techniques are used in Report design.

In the page footer area of a report, the page number is usually shown. The page number is placed in a Text Box. If you have created a report and it doesn't have the pages numbered, you can easily add page numbering in Design view.

1 If necessary, scroll down through your form until you see the Page Footer area.

2 Click the **Text Box** tool then click and drag in the Page Footer area to indicate the position of the Text Box.

- A Text Box field consists of a description (the left part) and a detail area (the right part).

3 Edit the text in the description (left) part of the text box, or delete the description – select it and press [**Delete**].

To put a page number in the detail part of the Text Box:

1 Select the box – click on it once.

2 Type =[**Page**] in the field.

Grouping

If you didn't use the wizard to specify grouping for a report, you can group (or ungroup) the records from Design view.

Grouping is specified in the **Sorting and Grouping** dialog box.

1 Click the **Sorting and Grouping** tool 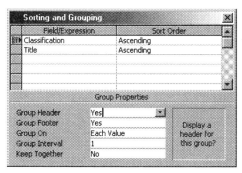 on the Report Design toolbar.

2 In the **Field/Expression** area – select the field you want to group on from the drop-down list, e.g. Town.

3 Set the **Sort Order**.

4 In the **Group Properties** pane set the **Group Header** to **Yes** (to put the name of the town at the top of each group).

5 Specify any other fields you want sorted in the dialog box.

6 Close the dialog box to return to your design grid.

7 Add fields, text, etc. as required into the group header and or footer.

Finishing touches

By using the Toolbox and the Formatting toolbar, you can add the finishing touches to the objects in your report (or form) by adding lines, borders, colour and special effects. There are instructions to help get you started in Chapter 3.

Summary

This chapter has discussed setting up and manipulating a database using Microsoft Access. Topics covered included:

* Planning and designing a database
* Database jargon and Access objects
* Primary Key
* Data types and properties
* Setting up and editing the table design
* Relationships
* Entering and editing data
* Formatting the datasheet
* AutoForm
* Form Design view
* Form Wizard
* Printing the datasheet
* Sorting data on single and multiple fields
* Using Find to locate records
* Extracting records using the Filter option
* Setting up and running a simple Query
* AutoReport
* Report Wizard
* Report Design view

07

presentations

In this chapter you will learn

- about PowerPoint and presentations
- how to create slides and handouts
- how to add tables and charts
- how to prepare and deliver a presentation

7.1 Introduction to PowerPoint

You can use PowerPoint to produce all you need for presentations:

Slides – the individual pages of a presentation. They may contain text, graphs, clip art, tables, drawings and animation, video clips, visuals from other applications – and more!! PowerPoint will allow you to present your slides via a slide show on your computer, 35mm slides or overhead projector transparencies.

Notes Pages – to accompany your slides. Each notes page has a small image of the slide plus any typed notes. You can print the pages and use them to prompt you during a presentation.

Handouts – smaller versions of your slides that can be printed 2, 3, 6 or 9 to a page. They provide backup material for your audience and can be customized with a company name or logo.

Outline – a useful overview of your presentation's structure, this has the slide titles and main text, but no art work or drawings.

Getting started

When you start PowerPoint a new blank presentation is created, with a blank Title slide, and the **New Presentation** Task Pane is displayed (unless the **Show at startup** checkbox has been deselected).

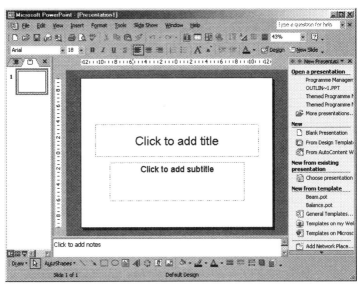

The boxes with dotted outlines that appear when you create a new slide are called placeholders.

The PowerPoint window is very similar to other Office application windows. The Standard and Formatting toolbars usually appear along the top of the window. The Drawing toolbar is usually along the bottom of the window.

If you are ready to start work on a new presentation, close the Task Pane so that there is more room for your work.

◆ You can keep the Task Pane displayed as you work if you prefer, it's really a matter of personal preference.

PowerPoint objects

The text and graphics that you can place on a slide in PowerPoint are called *objects*. An object may be:

◆ Text	◆ Drawings	◆ Graphs	◆ Tables
◆ WordArt	◆ Clip art	◆ Movies	◆ Sounds

◆ Organization Charts or other diagrams

Different slide layouts have different placeholders – these will contain the slide title, slide text and any other objects on your slide.

1 Follow the prompts on the slide – enter the title and sub-title (if required) for your presentation.

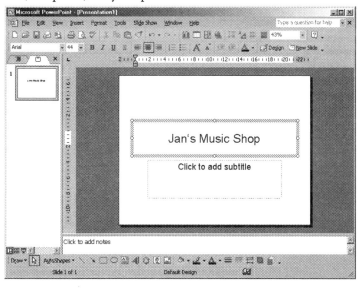

2 Click the New Slide tool.

3 Select a slide layout from the Slide Layout Task Pane (a single bulleted list layout is the default).

4 Enter your text – follow the prompts.

5 Repeat steps 2–4 until all slides have been added.

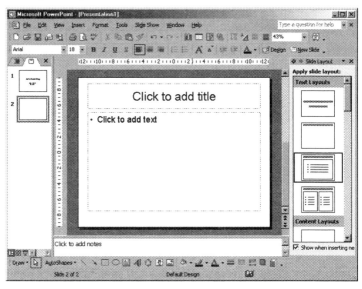

Things to note/experiment with:

*   To insert a new slide from the Slide Layout Task Pane, click the drop-down arrow to the right of the slide layout, then click **Insert New Slide**.

*   You can resize the Task Pane by clicking and dragging its left border.

*   Use the arrows at the top left of the Task Pane to move between the New Presentation and the Slide Layout Task Panes.

*   Scroll through the list of layouts to display the various types of layout, e.g. Text, Content, Text and Content and Other.

*   Some of the slide layouts in the Slide Layout Task Pane have graphic, table, organization chart and clip art objects set up on them. We will look at these later in the book.

7.2 Creating a new presentation

When the New Presentation Task Pane is displayed, you can create a new presentation in a number of ways.

- **Blank Presentation** creates a new blank presentation and displays the Slide Layout Task Pane (see above).

- **From Design Template** creates a new presentation and displays the Slide Design Task Pane so you can choose a template on which to base your presentation (the template will determine the design elements of you presentation, including font and colour scheme).

- **From AutoContent Wizard** creates a new presentation and starts a wizard to step you through the process of setting up your title slide, outline of presentation and colour scheme.

Design Template

To create a new presentation using the Design Template option:

1 Click **From Design Template** on the New Presentation Task Pane.

2 Select a template from those listed (or click **Browse...** and locate the template you wish to use).

3 Complete the Title Slide, e.g. Click to add title, click to add subtitle.

4 Click the ⊟New Slide tool on the Formatting toolbar.

5 Select the layout required for your next slide.

6 Follow the instructions on the slide to complete it.

7 Repeat steps 4–6 until all slides have been added.

If you don't like the look of your selected template, change it from the Slide Design Task Pane. To display this:

- Click the ⊘Design tool on the Formatting toolbar.

- Click the arrows at the top left of the Task Pane until the Slide Design Task Pane is displayed.

Or

- Double-click on the Template name on the Status bar.

AutoContent Wizard

The AutoContent Wizard sets up several slides – the exact number depends on the choices you make as you work through the Wizard. If you need help setting up the structure of your presentation, or need some ideas on what to put on your slides, this option may be useful.

1 Click **From AutoContent Wizard** on the Task Pane.

2 The first time you run the Wizard the Office Assistant dashes to your aid! Close it if you wish and click ▨▨▨▨.

3 Pick the option that best describes the type of presentation you are going to give.

4 Select the presentation style – on-screen, Web, overheads or slides.

5 Enter the presentation title and any information that you want displayed in the slide footer area.

6 At the last screen click ▨▨▨. PowerPoint will set up your presentation.

Working through the Wizard, click:

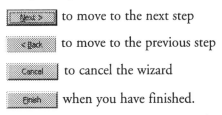

▨▨▨ to move to the next step

▨▨▨ to move to the previous step

▨▨▨ to cancel the wizard

▨▨▨ when you have finished.

• Once a presentation has been created (using any of the above options) you can easily add or delete slides, change slide layouts or change the design template used.

You can create a new blank presentation by clicking the **New** tool on the Standard toolbar, or by pressing [**Ctrl**]-[**N**].

• If you have closed the Task Pane, you can display the New Presentation Task Pane by opening the **File** menu and choosing **New...** or by opening the **View** menu and choosing **Task Pane**.

7.3 View options

When working on a presentation, there are three view options to choose from:

* Normal view
* Slide Sorter view
* Slide Show

By default, PowerPoint displays new presentations in Normal view.

Use the icons  at the bottom left of the screen to change the view of your presentation. You can also change views using the **View** menu.

The **View** menu has an additional option called *Notes Page view*. This displays a miniature of your slide, with the notes area below it, showing how your notes will look when printed. You can also enter and edit your notes in this view. If you wish to do this, use the **Zoom** tool on the Standard toolbar to zoom into about 75% so that you can read the text.

Jan's Music Shop

High Street
Dundee

Any notes that you want to make to prompt you during your presentation can be entered into the notes area.

In Slide Sorter view each slide is displayed in miniature – this view can be used for moving slides around and to help you prepare for the actual presentation. We will discuss this view later in the chapter.

Slide Show view can be useful at any time to let you see how your slide will look in the final presentation. Press [**Esc**] from Slide Show view to return to your presentation file.

The view that you will use when setting up your presentation is Normal view. In Normal view, you have three panes displaying different parts of your presentation. The slide itself is in the top right (the Slide Pane), notes are displayed in the bottom right (the Notes Pane) and the outline and slide tabs are displayed down the left (Outline and Slide Pane).

A Task Pane will often be displayed too.

Outline and Slides Pane

In Normal view the Outline and Slides Pane is displayed on the left of the screen.

The Outline tab displays the text on each slide, with a slide icon to the left of each slide title.

You can insert and delete text in the Outline tab just as you would on the Slide itself.

You can select a slide on the Outline tab by clicking the slide icon.

The Slide tab displays miniatures of the slides in your presentation.

Notes Pane

As the presenter, you may wish to add some notes (that you can use during your presentation) to some of your slides.

Notes are added to the Notes Pane, below the Slide Pane (or in Notes Pages view – see above).

To add notes to the Notes Pane:

1 Click in the Notes Pane.

2 Type in your notes.

Hide/Restore Panes

◆ Click the Close button at the top right of the Outline and Slides Pane to hide the pane.

Both the Outline and Slides Pane and the Notes Pane disappear.

◆ Click the Normal view icon or open the **View** menu and choose **Normal** (**Restore Panes**) to restore the pane.

You can resize the panes if you wish – click and drag the pane border to do so.

7.4 Working with slides

To move through the slides in your presentation:

◆ Click on the slide that you wish to display on the Slides tab.

Or

◆ Click the Next Slide or Previous Slide button at the bottom of the vertical scroll bar.

Or

◆ Drag the elevator on the vertical scroll bar up and down.

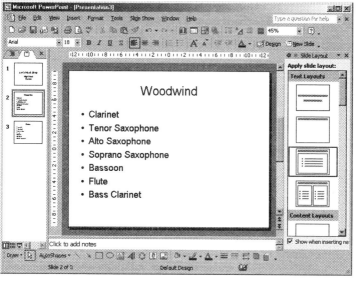

Once you've started your presentation, the next step is to decide on the text that you want on your slides – the title, and the main points that you want to discuss during your presentation.

The main text on a slide will be in the title or the bulleted list area.

You can determine the structure of the text on each slide (main points, sub-points, etc.), using up to 5 levels if necessary.

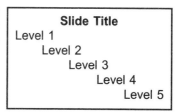

To edit text:

1   Locate the slide you want to edit.

2   Click to place the insertion point inside the text to be edited.

3   Insert or delete characters as required.

• If you want to change the text completely, select the old text (click and drag over it) and key in the replacement text.

To add new slides:

You can add new slides at any place in your presentation.

1   View the slide that you want above your new one.

2   Click the **New Slide** tool ⬚New Slide on the Standard toolbar (not the **New** tool).

3   Select a layout.

Structuring a slide

The points you want to make on your slides will be structured – you will have main points (at the first bulleted level) and some of these points will have sub-points (at the second, third, fourth or even fifth level). Initially, all points are at level 1. You can demote sub-items if necessary (and promote them again if you change your mind).

1   Place the insertion point within the item.

2   Click the **Increase Indent** tool ▦ on the Formatting toolbar.

Or

• Click the **Decrease Indent** tool ▦ on the Formatting toolbar.

Moving bullet points

You can easily rearrange the points on your slide using cut and paste or drag and drop techniques, or click inside the item you wish to move and press [**Shift**]-[**Alt**]-[↑] to move an item up, [**Shift**]-[**Alt**]-[↓] to move an item down.

To move slides:

• Drag and drop the slide miniatures to move the slides in either the Slide Pane in Normal view or in Slide Sorter view.

To delete slides:

1 Select the slide miniature in the Slide Pane in Normal view.

2 Press [**Delete**].

7.5 Formatting

Most of the formatting options, e.g. bold, alignment and bullets work in the same way as in all other applications. The formatting options covered here are unique to PowerPoint.

Changing a slide layout

If you decide you have chosen the wrong layout for a slide, it is easily changed.

1 View the slide whose layout you wish to change.

2 Display the Slide Layout Task Pane (use the arrow at the top of the Task Pane, or click the **Slide Layout** tool ![Layout]).

3 Select the layout required.

To increase/decrease paragraph spacing:

1 Select the paragraphs.

2 Click to increase ![icon] or decrease ![icon] the paragraph spacing to get your text evenly distributed on your slide.

♦ You'll find the tools on the Formatting toolbar under **Add or Remove buttons...** if they aren't already on the toolbar.

Changing the Design template

You can change your presentation design template at any time. This determines the design elements of your presentation – colour, fonts, alignment of text, etc.

1 Double-click the template name field on the Status bar.

Or

♦ Click ![Design] to display the Design Task Pane.

2 Select the template you want to use.

Background styles

When you select a template, the background colour and shading is picked up from its options. You can easily change the colour and shading while retaining the other design elements.

If your presentation were in sections, e.g. on individual departments or regional figures, you could set a different background colour for each section of your presentation.

1 Choose **Background...** from the **Format** menu.

2 Choose the **Background Fill** option from the list.

Or

3 To display more options, click **More Colors...** or **Fill Effects...** then set the options in the dialog boxes and click **OK**.

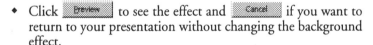

4 Click  to apply it to the selected slide or to apply to all slides in the presentation.

* Click to see the effect and if you want to return to your presentation without changing the background effect.

And yet more options...

Experiment with the other options in the **Format** menu. **Font**, **Bullets and Numbering**, **Alignment** and **Line Spacing** are very similar to those found in the other Office applications.

You can select several slides at once in Slide Sorter view then change the colours of them all in one operation.

* To select several adjacent slides in Slide Sorter view, click on the first one, then [**Shift**]-click on the last one that you wish to select.

* To select non-adjacent cells, click on the first one, and then hold [**Ctrl**] down while you click on each of the others.

7.6 Headers and footers

If you want to add slide numbers, the date, time or any other header or footer to your slide, notes or handouts use the Header and Footer command.

1 Open the **View** menu.

2 Choose **Header and Footer...**

3 Select the appropriate tab – **Slide** or **Notes and Handouts**.

4 Tick the items you want to appear, giving details as needed.

5 Click [Apply] or [Apply to All].

7.7 Charts

Charts can be useful if you have figures to present and feel that a graphical representation would be more effective than just the figures themselves.

There are three main ways to set up your chart:

Using a Chart placeholder

♦ Double-click within the Chart placeholder to add a chart.

Using a Content placeholder

♦ Click the Insert Chart tool within the placeholder.

From a slide with no placeholder set

♦ Click the Insert Chart tool 🔳 on the Standard toolbar.

Datasheet and toolbars

Regardless of how you decide to create your chart, Microsoft Graph opens and a chart window is displayed. This has its own Standard and Formatting toolbars, and you will notice a **Chart** menu on the Menu bar. The options available in the other menus change to ones suitable for working on charts.

There is also a small Datasheet window (which can be moved or resized as necessary), where you can key in the data that you want to chart. When working in Microsoft Graph the Help menu will give you access to Help pages on the program.

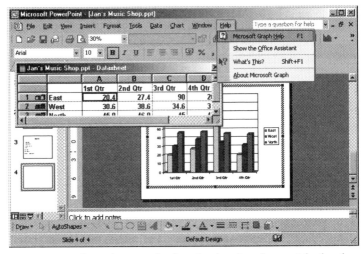

You must replace the sample data in the datasheet with the data you want to chart. If you do not need to replace all the data, delete the extra cell contents – select the column or row and press [Delete].

1 Select the cell into which you wish to enter your own data.

2 Key in the data.

3 Move to the next cell you want to work on – use any of the methods shown below.

To move from cell to cell in the datasheet with the keyboard:

Arrow keys	one cell in direction of arrow
[Tab]	forward to the next cell
[Shift]-[Tab]	back to the previous cell
[Enter]	down to the next cell in a column

To move with the mouse:

• Point to the cell and click

The cell you are in (your current cell) has a dark border.

View/hide datasheet

Once you have keyed in your data, you can hide the datasheet so you can see the chart clearly on your screen. If you hide your datasheet, you can easily view it again if you need to edit any data.

• Click the **View Datasheet** tool 🔳 on the Standard toolbar to view or hide the Datasheet, as required.

7.8 Chart options

By Row and By Column

The Category axis has labels taken from the column or row headings in your datasheet. Use the **By Row** 🔳 and **By Column** 🔳 tools to indicate whether your data series is in rows or columns. A graphic in the row or column heading of your datasheet indicates the selected option.

Chart type

The default chart type is a column chart. You can try out a variety of other chart types using the **Chart Type** tool on the Standard toolbar.

1 Click the drop-down arrow to display the chart types available.

2 Choose one.

• Open the **Chart** menu and choose **Chart Type...** You'll find lots of other options to choose from.

Hiding columns

If you don't want all your data to be displayed, you can hide rows or columns as required. This is done on the datasheet.

1 Display the datasheet if necessary.

2 Double-click on the heading of the column or row to hide.

• The data is dimmed, and is not displayed on your chart.

3 Double-click the heading again to unhide the column or row.

Colours and patterns

If you don't like the colour of a data series – the bars or lines representing one set of data – experiment with the options.

To change the colour of a data series:

1 With the chart selected, click on an item (e.g. bar or line) to select the series.

2   Click the **Fill Color** drop-down arrow on the Drawing toolbar.

3   Select a colour (or choose **Fill Effects** to display the dialog box and select from the gradients, textures and patterns).

To format any chart object:

1   Double-click on the object you wish to format.

2   Select the options from the **Formatting** dialog box.

3   Click **OK**.

Tour the options in the Formatting dialog boxes carefully. They are full of features that can help you make the most of your chart!

Chart title and axis legends

To add a chart title or axis legend:

1   Open the **Chart** menu and choose **Chart Options**.

2   Select the **Titles** tab.

3   Enter the titles as required and click **OK**.

To edit the title or legends:

1   Click the object once to select it.

2   Click again to place the insertion point within the text.

3   Edit as usual.

4   Click outside the object when finished.

To format the title or legend:

1   Click the object once to select it.

2   Use the tools on the Formatting toolbar.

Or

◆ Double-click on the object to open its **Format** dialog box.

To delete the title or legends:

1   Click the object once to select it.

2   Press [**Delete**].

Use the Text Box and Arrow tools on the Drawing toolbar to add emphasis to your charts.

Exiting Microsoft Graph

* When your chart is complete, click anywhere on the slide outside the chart placeholder to return to your presentation.

The whole chart becomes an object within your presentation, and can be moved, copied, deleted or resized as necessary.

* If you wish to edit your chart, simply double-click on it.

7.9 Organization charts

Organization charts give you another opportunity to make your point using a diagram rather than words. There are three main ways to set up your organization chart.

From a slide with the Diagram placeholder:

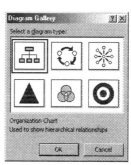

1 Double-click within the placeholder on your slide.

2 Select **Organization Chart** from the **Diagram Gallery** dialog box.

3 Click **OK**.

From a slide with a Contents placeholder:

1 Click the **Insert Diagram or Organization Chart** tool within the placeholder.

2 Select **Organization Chart** from the **Diagram Gallery** dialog box and click **OK**.

From a slide with no placeholder:

1 Click the **Insert Diagram or Organization Chart** tool on the Drawing toolbar.

2 Select **Organization Chart** from the **Diagram Gallery** dialog box and click **OK**.

An organization chart object will be displayed on your slide.

Work out the structure you wish to display before you start. Don't try to display too large a structure – the finished slide should be clear and easy to understand.

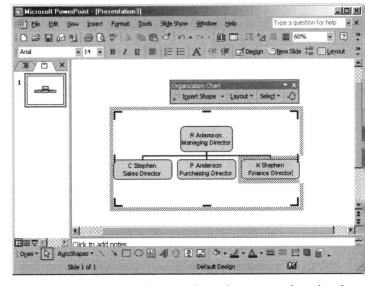

Organization charts can be complicated structures but they have only simple elements. The small set of tools in the Organization Chart toolbar is all that you need.

Text and boxes

To enter text into a box:

1 Click in the box you wish to edit.

2 Key in your data and press [**Enter**] or the arrow keys to move to the next row.

3 Click on the next box to be completed, or anywhere outside the box, when you are finished.

To add a box:

1 Click on the box to which the new box is related.

2 Click **Insert Shape** on the Organization Chart toolbar.

3 Select the box type required.

To delete a box:

1 Click on the edge of the box to select it.

2 Press [**Delete**].

Layout

The default layout for an organization chart is the Standard one. You can easily change the layout for all or part of a chart.

To change the layout:

1 Select a 'manager' box – one that has subordinates.

2 Click **Layout** on the Organization Chart toolbar.

3 Select the layout option required.

To select a set of boxes:

1 Select one of the boxes required.

2 Click **Select** on the Organization Chart toolbar.

3 Choose the group of boxes from the options available.

Autoformat

To quickly format the whole of your chart effectively:

1 Click the **Autoformat** tool on the Organization Chart toolbar.

2 Select an Autoformat.

3 Click **Apply**.

◆ Click outside the Organization Chart placeholder when you have finished.

7.10 Tables

If you have created tables using Word, you'll find it very easy to create them on your slides. The options for creating a table are similar to those for a graph or organization chart.

1 Select a slide layout with a Table or Content placeholder on it.

2 Click the **Insert Table** tool.

3 Specify the number of rows and columns required.

4 Click **OK**.

On a slide without a placeholder:

1 Click the **Insert Table** tool.

2 Drag over the grid to indicate the number of rows and columns required.

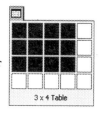

3 x 4 Table

The Tables and Borders toolbar will appear when a table is selected.

- If it doesn't appear, click the **Tables and Borders** tool .

When working in a table:

- Press [**Tab**] to move to the next cell, [**Shift**]-[**Tab**] to go back to the previous cell or use the arrow keys to between cells.

Or

- Click in the cell you wish to work on.
- Click outside the table when you've finished.
- Click on your table again if you wish to edit it.

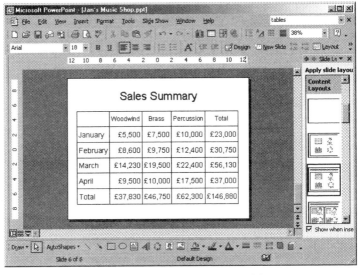

- *See section 4.15 for more information on tables.*

7.11 The Clip Gallery

PowerPoint comes with hundreds of clip art pictures that can be added to your slides. You'll also find many more on the Internet.

To insert clip art into a slide:

1 Click the **Insert Clip Art** tool on the Drawing toolbar.

2   Enter your search keywords, e.g. food, music, animal.

3   Click on the picture required.

4   Move/resize the clip art as required.

To insert clip art onto a slide with a Content or Clip Art placeholder:

1   Click on the **Insert Clip Art** tool in the Content placeholder, or double-click the Clip Art placeholder.

2   Enter your search keywords, e.g. food, music, animal.

3   Click on the picture required.

◆ *See section 3.12 for more on inserting clip art.*

7.12 Masters

Masters are the templates on which slides, handouts and notes pages are based. They contain information on fonts, placeholder sizes and positions, background design and colour schemes. Slide masters are used to set global formatting, or to add/remove a logo or picture which will affect all the slides in the presentation.

A Slide Master is added to a presentation any time you apply a Design template. Most design templates have a Slide Master and a Title Master. These are displayed as miniatures in the Slide Pane when you view a master.

Slide Master

The Slide Master holds the formatted placeholders for the slide title and text. Any slides where you have made changes to the text formatting, etc. will be treated as exceptions and will retain the custom formatting you applied to them.

Any objects you want to appear on every slide (e.g. a company name or logo) should be added to the Slide Master.

1   Choose **Master** from the **View** menu.

2   Select **Slide Master**.

3   Amend the Slide Master as required (using the same techniques that you use on a slide in your presentation).

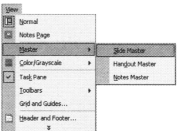

4 Choose an alternative view to leave your Slide Master.

• If you hold down [**Shift**] and click the Slide View 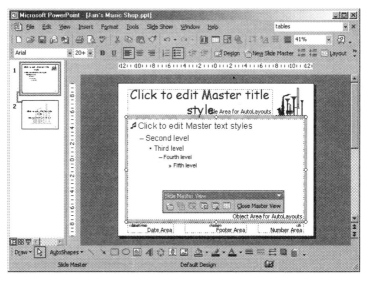 button, this takes you to the Slide Master, or to the Title Master if you are on the Title Slide at the time.

If you have no title master in your presentation you can easily add one (the Blank Presentation option has no master title):

1 View the Slide Master.

2 Click the **Insert New Title Master** tool on the Slide Master View toolbar.

The placeholders

The Object Areas for AutoLayouts, Date Area, Footer Area or Number Area placeholders are all optional. They can easily be deleted – or put back again if you decide you want them after all.

To delete a placeholder:

• Select the placeholder and press [**Delete**].

To restore a placeholder:

1 Click the **Master Layout** tool.

2 Select the placeholders required and click **OK**.

• To leave Master view, select any other view.

7.13 Slide Shows

The whole point of setting up a presentation is so that you can eventually deliver it to your audience. Once you've got your slides organized, there are a number of tools you can use to help you finalize your preparations.

Slide Sorter view

There are several useful features worth exploring in Slide Sorter view, including: hiding slides, setting up transitions, animating text on slides and rehearsing timings.

• Click the **Slide Sorter view** tool 🔡.

Slide Sorter toolbar

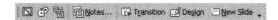

Hide Slide

This option can prove useful if you're not sure if you really need a particular slide for your presentation. You can include the slide (in case it's needed), but hide it. The hidden slide will be bypassed during your slide show, unless you decide you need to use it.

1 Select the slide you want to hide.

2 Click the **Hide Slide** tool 🔲.

• The slide number is crossed out under the slide

• If you want to show the hidden slide during a presentation press [**H**] at the slide preceding the hidden one.

• To remove the hidden status from a slide, select it and click the **Hide Slide** tool again.

Rehearse timings

It is a very good idea to practise your presentation before you end up in front of your audience. As well as practising what you in-tend to say (probably with the aid of notes you have made using the Notes Pages feature), you can rehearse the timings for each slide.

1 Click the **Rehearse Timings** tool 🔲 to go into your slide show for a practice run.

2 Go over what you intend to say while the slide is displayed.

3 Click to move to the next slide when ready.

4 Repeat steps 2 and 3 until you reach the end of your presentation.

A dialog box displays the total time of your presentation and asks if you want to record and use the timings in a slide show. Choose **Yes**, if you want each slide to advance after the allocated time.

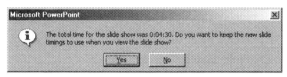

The slide timings will be displayed in Slide Sorter view.

• You can rehearse your timings as often as is necessary, until you've got the pace right to get your message across.

Summary Slide

You can get PowerPoint to automatically produce a Summary Slide for your presentation. The Summary Slide is placed in front of the other slides and holds a list of the titles of the selected slides.

1 Select the slides from which you wish to produce a Summary Slide.

2 Click the **Summary Slide** tool 🖼️ on the Slide Sorter toolbar.

• PowerPoint will generate as many Summary Slides as is necessary to list the title detail from all the slides you select.

Notes

You can also add notes to your slides from Slide Sorter view.

1 Click the **Notes** tool 🖼️Notes to open the **Notes** dialog box.

2 Select the slide that you wish to add or edit notes for.

3 Enter or edit the notes as required.

4 Repeat steps 2–3 for each slide as required.

5 Close the dialog box when you've finished.

Transitions

A transition is an effect used when a slide appears in a show. The default is that no transition is set, but there are several interesting alternatives that you might find effective for your presentation.

1 Select the slide that you wish to give a transition effect.

2 Click the **Slide Transition** tool.

• The Slide Transition Task Pane is displayed.

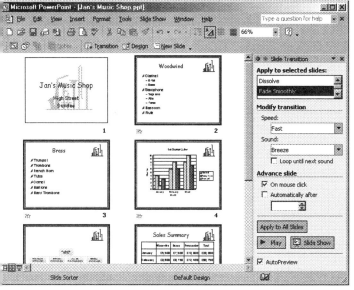

3 Select the effect required from the list (it will preview if AutoPreview is selected at the bottom of the Task Pane).

4 Set the **Speed** to *Fast*. Focus your audience on your slides, not the transition method!

5 Select a **Sound** if you wish.

6 Choose an **Advance slide** option.

• **Apply to Master** saves the effect in the Slide Master. All new slides added to the presentation will have the transition effect.

• **Apply to All** applies the effect to all the slides, not just the selected one(s). New slides will not have the transition effect.

• **Play** previews the effect on the selected slide.

• **Slide Show** displays the slide and effect in Slide Show view.

If a transition is set, a transition icon appears below the slide in Slide Sorter view. Click on it to see the effect.

Animation

If you have several points listed in the body text of your slide, you could try building the slide up, rather than presenting the whole list at once. Experiment with the Animation options and effects until you find the ones you prefer. You can have a lot of fun with the options – but avoid having a different effect on each slide!

To set an animation effect:

1 Click the **Design** tool ![Design] to display the Design Task Pane.

2 Select **Animation Schemes** on the Slide Design Task Pane.

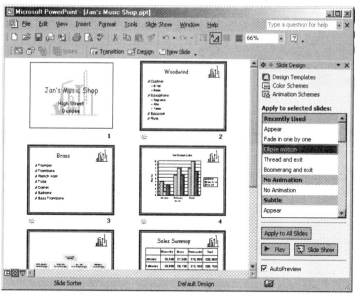

3 Select the slide(s) you wish to animate.

4 Pick an effect from the list.

5 Click **Apply to Master** or **Apply to All Slides**.

6 Close the Task Pane when you have made your settings.

- With your slide selected in Slide Sorter view, click the Slide Show icon, work through your slide then press [**Esc**] to return to Slide Sorter view.

7.14 Slide Show

You can run your slide show at any time to check how your presentation is progressing. Each slide fills the whole of your screen. After the last, you are returned to the view you were in when you clicked the **Slide Show** tool.

1   Select the slide you want to start from, usually the first.

2   Click the **Slide Show** icon 🔲 to the left of the horizontal scroll bar.

3   Press [**Page Down**] or [**Enter**] (or click the left mouse button) to move onto the next slide.

- Press [**Page Up**] to move back to the previous slide if necessary.
- You can exit your slide show at any time by pressing [**Esc**].

When presenting your slide show, you might want to go directly to a slide, or draw on a slide to focus attention. These, and other features, can be accessed using the pop-up menu or the keyboard.

To open the menu:

1   Right-click anywhere on the screen or click the pop-up menu icon 🖉◁ at the bottom left corner.

To go directly to a slide:

2   Select **Go**, then **By Title**.

3   Choose the slide you want to go to.

- Explore the options on the pop-up menu.

To draw on your screen:

1   Press [**Ctrl**]-[**P**] to change the mouse pointer to a pen.

2   Click and drag to draw.

3   Press [**Ctrl**]-[**A**] to change the pointer back to an arrow.

To erase your drawing:

4   Press [**E**] on your keyboard.

- To get more help on the options available to you while running Slide Show, press [F1]. The **Slide Show Help** dialog box lists other options you might want to experiment with.

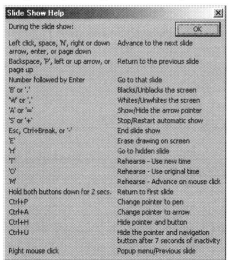

7.15 Printing presentations

You can print your whole presentation – the slides, speaker's notes pages, audience handouts and the presentation outline.

The first stage to printing is to set up the format.

1 Choose **Page Setup** from the **File** menu.

2 Select the size from the **Slides sized for** field.

3 Specify the orientation required for the **Slides**.

4 Specify the orientation required for the **Notes, handouts & outline**.

5 Click **OK**.

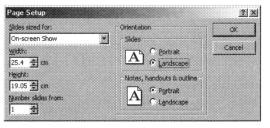

Printing

With the Page Setup details specified to give the output required, you can go ahead and print. If you click the Print icon, one copy of each slide is printed. To print anything else you must access the **Print** dialog box and specify what you want to print.

1 Open the **File** menu and choose **Print**.

2 Specify the **Print range** to print – *All, Current Slide, Selection* or specified *Slides*.

3 Select the option required in the **Print what:** list.

   Slides – prints your slides one slide per page.

   Handouts – prints miniatures of the slides 2, 3, 4, 6 or 9 to the page. Printing your handouts with 3 slides to the page is particularly useful as there is room for your audience to make their own notes.

   Notes Pages – prints a slide miniature on each page, together with any notes that you have made to prompt you during your presentation.

   Outline View – prints the text of each slide, showing the structure of the presentation.

4 Specify any other options required.

5 Click **OK**.

Summary

In this chapter you found out how to create a presentation using PowerPoint. We have discussed:

+ The content of a presentation file – slides, handouts, notes, outline

+ Creating a new presentation

+ Adding slides to the presentation

+ Slide layout

+ Design Templates

+ The structure of bullet points

+ Charts

+ Organization charts

+ Tables

+ The Clip Gallery

+ Masters

+ Hide slide, rehearse timings, summary slide, notes, transition effects and slide animation

+ Giving a presentation

+ Printing the presentation file

08

internet and e-mail

In this chapter you will learn

- how to surf the Web
- how to customize Internet Explorer
- how to manage favorites
- about search engines
- how to use Hotmail
- how to send attachments
- about managing your messages and contacts

8.1 First steps with the Internet

To open your browser:

◆ Double-click the Internet Explorer shortcut on your Desktop.

Or

◆ Click the **Launch Internet Explorer Browser**  icon on the Taskbar.

If you have a dial-up connection (one where you connect to your Internet Service Provider (ISP), and through them to the Internet over the public telephone lines) you'll be asked for your user name and password.

◆ Complete the dialog box as necessary.

The page that appears on your screen when you open your browser application is your *Home Page*. This is also the one that you are returned to when you click .

Web addresses

A *web page* is a screen display that may contain text, graphics, sound, etc. A web site is a collection of linked pages holding the information for an individual or organization.

The URL (Uniform Resource Locator) is the address of the page you wish to visit. What do the URLs mean?

http:// identifies the address as a hypertext (web page) URL

www is how WWW (World Wide Web) addresses usually start (but not always, e.g. http://news.bbc.co.uk/)

Some URLs are very short, e.g. http://www.coke.com/

This address takes you to the website of CocaCola, a commercial organization in the USA.

Others are more complex, e.g. http://www.bbc.co.uk/scotland/education/bitesize/physics/electricity/

You will find URLs everywhere – in the press, on TV, on goods, etc. Make a note of any interesting ones so that you can visit them.

* If you know the URL of a web page that you wish to visit, simply key it into the **Address** field and press [**Enter**].

Home page

The home page is the one that appears when you start Internet Explorer. You should set it to one that you use regularly, e.g. your favourite search engine or your own web page.

To change the Home Page:

1 Locate the page you wish to use for your Home Page.

2 Open the **Tools** menu and choose **Internet Options…**

3 Select the **General** tab.

4 Click **Use Current** in the **Home Page** area.

5 Click **OK**.

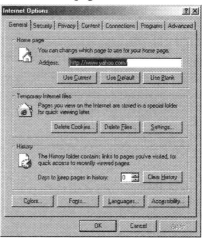

Saving a web page

If you find a page that you want to be able to view or print later when you are not connected to the Internet, you should save it.

1 Open the **File** menu.

2 Choose **Save As…**

3 Specify the drive/folder that you want the page on.

4 Accept or edit the file name.

5 Specify the **Save as** type option.

6 Click **Save**.

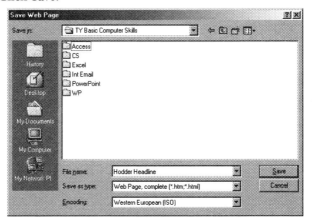

Help

The Help system is very similar to the Help in Windows and other applications. The Help menu gives you access to various Help areas.

You'll find more information on Help in Chapter 3.

To close the web browser:

◆ Click the Close button at the right of the title bar and disconnect from your ISP (unless you are connected to a LAN).

8.2 Browser settings

You can customize the way that your browser window looks by selecting from the various view options.

You can elect to display various Explorer bars to help you with your work. The Explorer bars are Favorites, Search and History.

To display an Explorer bar:

♦ Click the appropriate tool to open it in the Explorer bar.

Here, the Explorer bar is displaying Favorites

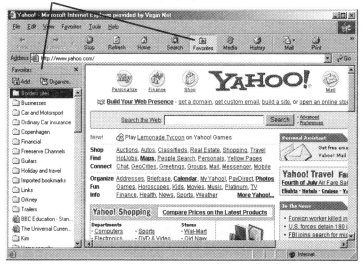

Toolbars

The toolbars that are normally displayed are the Standard buttons and the Address bar. There is also a Links bar.

To switch a toolbar on or off:

1 Open the **View** menu.

2 Choose **Toolbars**.

3 Select or deselect the toolbar as required.

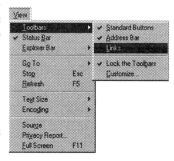

If the toolbars are not 'locked', you will see a raised handle to the left of the toolbar. You can move your toolbars by dragging these handles.

- You can toggle the 'locked' status of the toolbars in the **View > Toolbars** menu.

Customizing toolbars

You can customize the Standard toolbar.

1 Open the **View** menu, choose **Toolbars** then click **Customize...**

Or

- Right-click on a toolbar, then choose **Toolbars** and click **Customize...** on the shortcut menu.

2 **Add** or **Remove** tools from the lists as required.

3 To adjust the order, use the **Move Up** and **Move Down** buttons.

4 Specify the **Text options** and **Icon options**.

5 Close the dialog box when you've finished.

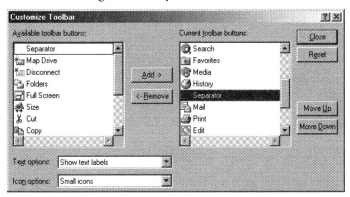

Display/hide images

Most web pages have pictures on them. Some pages are slow to download because of the pictures – the files are so big that it takes time to transfer them to your PC. To speed up the display of your web pages, you can turn the graphics off.

To switch off graphics:

1 Open the **Tools** menu and choose **Internet Options...**

2 Click the **Advanced** tab.

3 In the **Multimedia** area, deselect the **Show pictures** option (and/ or **Play animations, Play videos** or **Play sounds** as required).

◆ You can display an individual picture or animation on a page even if you have deselected the **Show pictures** or **Play videos** options. Right-click on its icon and then click **Show Picture**.

◆ If you wish to set up your system to display pictures again, repeat steps 1–3, selecting the checkboxes required.

If a page is taking a long time to download you may want to stop it – click the ⬛ **Stop** button if you do.

If a page isn't displaying correctly (or if it might have been updated since you last visited), click the ⬛ **Refresh** button to redraw it.

8.3 Web navigation

If you know the URL of the web page or site that you require you can easily go to it.

1 Enter its URL in the **Address** field.
2 Press [**Enter**].

Hyperlinks

Many of the pages that you visit will have hyperlinks to other pages or sites that you may be interested in. A hyperlink lets you

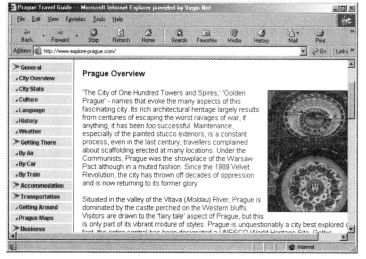

jump from one place on a page to another or from one page to another, or to a different site altogether.

A text hyperlink is usually coloured blue with a blue underline.

A hyperlink may also be a picture – if you pause the mouse pointer over a picture hyperlink, the pointer becomes a pointing hand.

• To jump to the location that the hyperlink points to, simply click on it.

As you jump from one location to another following the hyperlinks that interest you, you are *surfing* the net.

As you surf, you may want to revisit pages or sites you have already been to.

• Click the 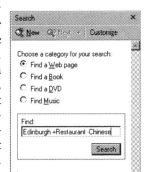 **Back** and **Forward** tools to move between the pages you've already visited.

Or

• Click and select the page you wish to return to.

8.4 Searching the Web

If you don't know the URL of a page or site you will need to search for it, and you can do this by using keywords – words which describe what you are looking for. The result of a search is a list of several (often thousands) of pages or sites that may be relevant.

To search using Explorer's Search facility:

1 Click to display the Search panel.

2 Chose a category – **Find a Web page**.

3 Enter the keyword(s) to search for – the more information you give, the more appropriate the results will be. For example, to find restaurants in Edinburgh, but not Chinese ones, enter '+Edinburgh +Restaurant -Chinese' in the Search field. A + (plus) means that the page must contain that word, a - (minus)means that the page must not contain the word.

4   Click **Search**.

Your search results will be displayed.

Search engines

Alternatively, you could try one of the many search engines, such as Yahoo (http://www.yahoo.com), AskJeeves (http://www.ask.co.uk), AltaVista (http://www.altavista.com) or Excite (http://www.excite.com). The one used in this example is Yahoo!.

Most search engines have a directory to allow you to locate the information you require by working through the various topics. However, if you know what you're looking for it's usually quicker to *search*. In Yahoo! you can specify the keywords and phrases in the **Search the Web:** field.

In this example the search is for short breaks in Speyside. Sites that have details of camping are not required, but I want to find sites that mention skiing.

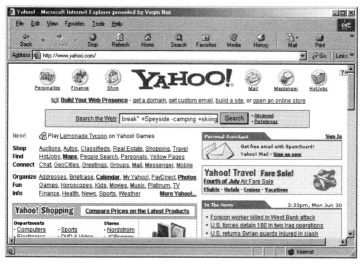

You will notice that:

◆ Phrases are enclosed within double quotes, e.g. "short breaks".

◆ Words that should be included are preceded by a plus, e.g. +Speyside.

◆ Words to be excluded are preceded by a minus, e.g. -camping.

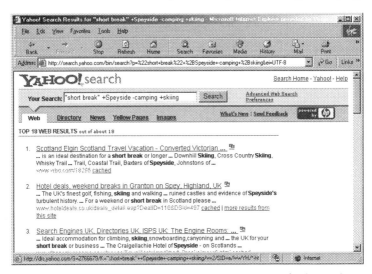

Look through the list of sites found – you may find you have hundreds of thousands of them (if this is the case you need to be much more precise in stating your search requirements). The search here turned up 18 sites.

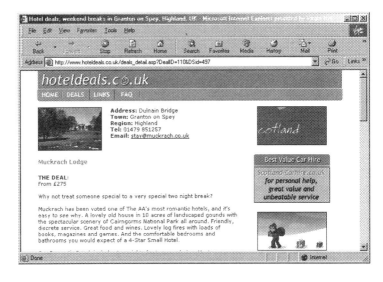

8.5 Favorites

If you find a site that you know you will want to revisit, you should add it to your list of favorites. You can then access the site easily without having to enter the URL or search it out.

1 Display the page that you want to add to your list of favorites.

2 Click on the Standard toolbar to display the Favorites panel.

3 Click **Add** at the top of the panel.

4 Edit the page name in the **Name** field if you wish.

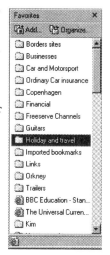

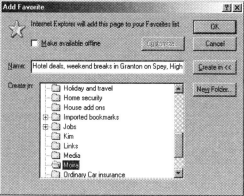

5 Select the folder that you want to add your page to.

6 Click **OK**.

To go to a page in your favorites list:

1 Display the **Favorites** panel.

2 Open the folder that contains your favorite.

3 Click on the page required.

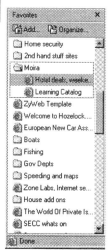

As you use the Internet your list of favorites will most probably get larger. If necessary you can set up folders to help you organize your favorites and move or delete them as necessary.

To create a new folder:

1 Click **Organize...** at the top of the Favorites panel.

2 At the **Organize Favorites** dialog box, click **Create Folder**.

3 Give your folder a name.

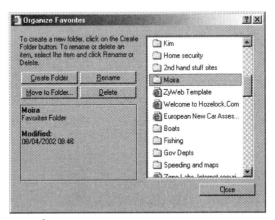

To rename an item:

1 Select it.

2 Click **Rename**.

3 Type in a new name.

4 Press [**Enter**].

To move an item:

1 Select it.

2 Click **Move to Folder...**

3 Select the folder you wish to move it to.

4 Click **OK**.

To delete an item:

1 Select it.

2 Click **Delete**.

3 Click **Yes** to confirm the deletion.

Collecting data and pictures for research

If you find a web page that contains data that would be useful for a report, or essay that you are working on you can collect the data in a Word document. As you work you may collect information from many different sources and add them to your document.

To copy text:

1 Select the text that you require from a web page.

2 Open the **Edit** menu and choose **Copy**.

3 Go to or open Word.

4 Create or open a document to paste your text into.

5 Position the insertion point where you want the text.

6 Click the **Paste** tool.

You can add more information to your document as you find it, edit the text, save the document and print it as required.

To copy a picture:

1 Right-click on the picture.

2 Click on **Copy**.

3 Go to the file that you want the copy to appear in.

4 Paste the picture.

Plagiarism

Be aware of plagiarism when using information from the Web (using other people's work and passing it off as your own). Although other people's work can be a useful resource, you should acknowledge your sources. There are many sites that give information on plagiarism.

Do a search on "plagiarism", or visit the site: http://www.cheathouse.com/.

And remember, your teachers and lecturers are becoming increasingly skilled at detecting plagiarism in papers!

8.6 Printing

If you find a web page that you would like to print you can do so easily.

You might want to check or change the page set up options.

1 Open the **File** menu.

2 Choose **Page Setup**.

3 Edit the fields as required, e.g. change the orientation or page size.

4 Click **OK**.

To preview a page before printing, open the **File** menu and choose **Print Preview**.

To print a page:

1 Click the **Print** tool on the Standard toolbar.

Or

2 Open the **File** menu and choose **Print**.

3 Set the Print options, e.g. page range, selection, frame, number of copies, etc.

4 Click **OK**.

8.7 E-mail

How did we live without e-mail? It's one of the quickest, cheapest ways to communicate (once you've got yourself set up with a computer with Internet access).

The convenience and flexibility of e-mail makes it a very attractive medium. You can send your messages and read the messages that you've received, at a time that suits you. Even if you are in a different time zone from those you communicate with, you don't need to wake anyone in the middle of the night to talk to them – just send them an e-mail and they'll get it when they next log on.

If you have a web-based e-mail account, you can send and receive your messages from anywhere in the world with Internet access – handy for those who globetrot! It has to be one of the best ways to keep in touch with family, friends and colleagues (next to meeting them for lunch!).

There are several web-based e-mail providers to choose from – many offering a free e-mail service.

* If you don't already have an e-mail account, and would like a free web-based one, visit http://www.emailaddresses.com to get a comparison of the current offerings.

The e-mail service discussed here is Hotmail. If you don't have a Hotmail account you can go to http://www.hotmail.com and set one up for yourself.

When you arrive in Hotmail your screen will look similar to this:

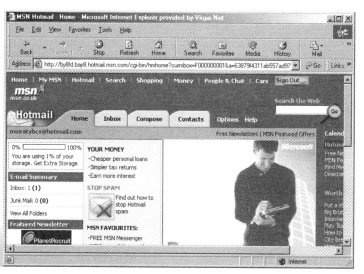

Things to be aware of:

* You may become a target for unsolicited e-mails – just as you may get telephone calls from salespeople, etc., you may also get rogue e-mails.

* You can minimize your exposure to this by ensuring that your security settings are set to limit it. Read the setup screens carefully when you subscribe to your e-mail service – you may be able to specify your preferences for incoming mail there. Go into **Options** in Hotmail and check/adjust your **Mail Handling** preferences as necessary.

* Viruses can be transmitted via e-mail attachments, so be cautious. Hotmail will check your attachments automatically.

8.8 Send a message

1 Select the **Compose** tab.

2 Enter the address of the recipient in the **To:** field (or click on their name in the **Quick Address List**).

3 If you wish to send a copy of the message to someone else, enter their address in the **Cc:** field.

4 Type in a **Subject**.

5 Key in your message.

6 Spell check your message – click the drop down arrow to the right of **Tools** (above your message) and choose **Spell Check**.

7 Select the *Copy Message to Sent Folder* checkbox if you wish to keep a copy for reference.

8 Click **Send**.

◆ A message will appear confirming that your message has been sent.

9 If you wish to save the address to your address book, select the **Save Address** checkbox, click **Save** and complete the details as required (see section 8.11 for more on the Address Book).

10 Click **Return to Inbox**.

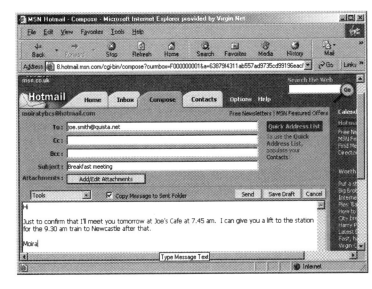

To:, Cc: and Bcc:

Type the address of each recipient into the appropriate field (if there is more than one address, separate them with a comma)

- The **To:** field is for the main recipient(s).

- To **Cc:** field is for those that you want to send a copy to so they know what's going on.

- The **Bcc:** field is for sending someone a *blind* copy. Only the message sender and the individual (or each individual) in the Bcc: field know to whom the message has been sent.

Subject field

Type the message title in the **Subject** field – this will be displayed in the Inbox of the recipient, so they have an idea what the message is about.

Message area

Type your message in here. You can format the text using the formatting tools at the top of the message area if you wish.

- Practise sending messages to some of your friends and family.

- You can copy and paste text from other e-mails or documents into your e-mail using normal copy and paste routines.

- If you opt to save a copy of the message that you send it will be listed in your *Sent Messages* folder.

- You can preview and print a message that you compose in the normal way – using the **Print** tool on the Standard toolbar, or from the **File** menu.

Signature

A signature is your standard way of closing your e-mail. It is automatically appended to your outgoing messages. You might like to finish your e-mails with something like:

With best wishes

Moira

Rather than type this into every message, you can automate the process.

1 Click **Options**.

2 Select **Signature** in the **Additional Options** list.

3 Show the rich-text toolbar if you want to format your text or add an *emoticon* (a tiny cartoon formed from characters, e.g. :-) is the standard 'smiley').

4 Enter and format your message.

5 Click **OK**.

• Next time you compose an e-mail, your signature will be added automatically.

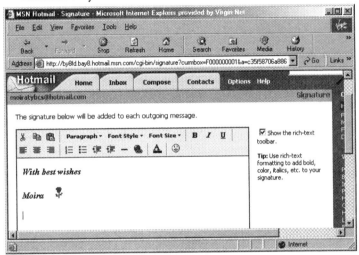

8.9 Inbox

Messages that you receive will be displayed in your Inbox.

Things to note about your Inbox:

• Unread messages have an envelope icon beside them, read messages have no envelope.

• If you have read a message, then want to mark it as unread again (perhaps to remind yourself to have another look at it), click the checkbox beside it and click **Mark as Unread**. The envelope icon will appear beside it again.

• You can **Sort** the messages in your Inbox into ascending or descending order. Click the column heading – **From**, **Subject**, **Date** or **Size** – to sort your messages.

• You can be selective about the e-mails you have listed in your Inbox – choose an option from the **Show me e-mail from** list.

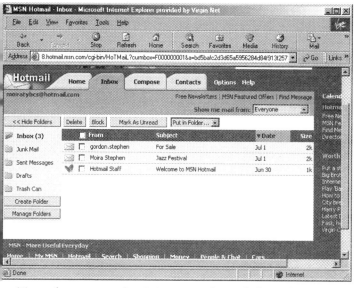

- To read a message that is in your Inbox, click on the name in the **From** column.

The message will be displayed on your screen.

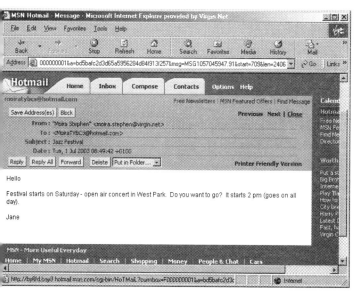

- You can save the address of the sender from here if you wish – click the **Save Address(es)** button above the **From** field in the header area.

- If you have received the e-mail from someone that you don't want to receive e-mails from, click the **Block** button (above the **From** field) and respond to the junk mail filter as appropriate. You can also block a message from the Inbox.

Print a message

You can print a copy of the e-mail you receive if you wish.

1 Open the message.

2 Click **Printer Friendly Version** above the message.

3 Open the **File** menu and choose **Print**.

4 Complete the dialog box as required.

5 Click **OK**.

6 Click the **Back** button on the Standard toolbar to return to your original message.

- To close a message without replying to it click **Close**.

Reply to/Forward a message

1 Open the message (if necessary).

2 To reply to a message, click **Reply** or **Reply All** when your message is displayed on the screen.

Or

- To Forward a message to someone else, click **Forward**

3 Enter the address details as required.

4 Type in your reply/message.

5 Click **Send**.

When you reply to a message, you can include the original message or you can just send your reply (without the original).

To include/not include the original message:

1 Click **Options** (when your message is displayed on the screen).

2 In the **Additional Options** column, click **Reply-Related Settings**

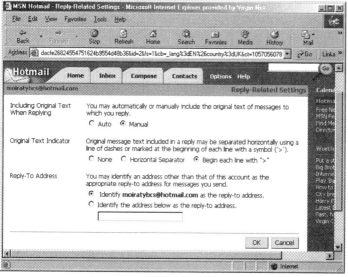

3 Select **Auto** (if you want the original message included) or **Manual** (if you just want to send your reply) at the **Including Original Text When Replying** option.

4 Click **OK**. You will be returned to the Options screen.

5 Choose the **Inbox/Compose** tab as required.

8.10 Attachments

You can attach files to an e-mail message. You may want to send someone a report or spreadsheet, or a holiday snap. But note that large attachments, e.g. pictures, can take a while to transmit.

To attach a file to a message:

1 Enter the address(es) and **Subject** fields as usual.

2 Click **Add/Edit Attachments** when your message is displayed.

3 At the **Attachments** screen, type in the file location and name (or click **Browse…** and locate the file you wish to send).

4 Click **Attach** to add your file to the list of attachments.

5 Repeat steps 2–3 until the required files have been attached.

6 Click **OK**. The attachments will be listed below the **Subject**.

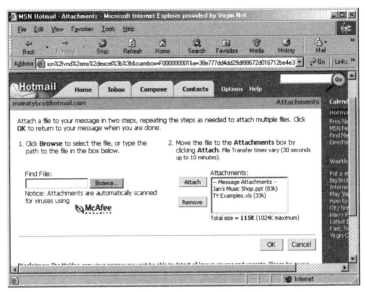

7 Enter your message (if you haven't already done so).

8 Spell check your message.

9 Copy it to the *Sent* folder (if you want to keep a copy).

10 Send your message.

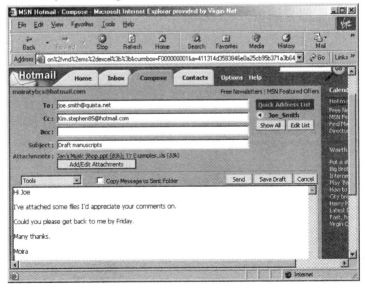

Saving an attachment

Some of the e-mails you receive will have attachments. You can open these files from their location in Hotmail, or download them and save them on your own computer.

To save an attachment on your own computer:

1. Open the e-mail.

2. Click on the Attachment name in the header area.

   Hotmail will scan the file for viruses. If no virus is found, you can download.

3. Click **Download file**.

4. At the **File Download** dialog box, click **Save**.

   Specify where you want the file saved – the default location is *My Download Files* on the C: drive.

5. When the download is complete you can open the file from your own drive.

Beware of attachments from unknown sources. Although Hotmail scans all attachments for viruses, there is no guarantee that it will catch everything. If in doubt, don't do it!

8.11 Address Book

It is a good idea to put addresses that you will use again into your Address Book. Then you can use them without having to re-key them. You can add addresses when you send a message (see section 8.8) or receive a message (see section 8.9), or you can enter them manually.

To add an address manually:

1. Select the **Contacts** tab.

2. Complete the **Quick Contact** details in the left pane.

Or

3. Click **New Contact**.

   Complete the *Required* information, e.g. Quickname.

   Complete the *Optional* information as you wish.

4. Click **OK** (at the bottom of details).

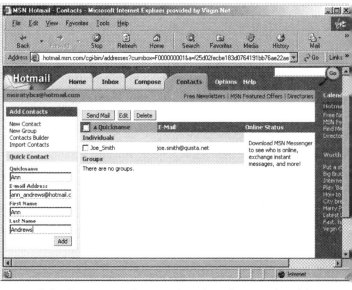

You will find your **Quicknames** listed in the **Quick Address List**
at the top right of the Compose screen when you write a message.

You can also set up 'distribution lists' or Groups, so that you can
quickly address your e-mails.

1   Select the **Contacts** tab.

2   Click **New Group** in the **Add Contacts** list.

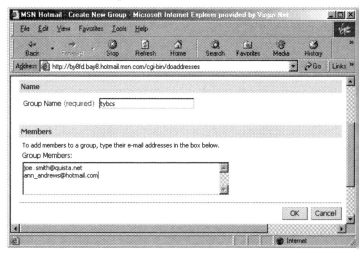

3 Enter a name for your Group.

4 Add the e-mail addresses of those who will be in the group.

5 Click **OK**.

* To send an e-mail to the group, simply type the group name into the **To:** field in your message.

8.12 Message management

Once you've started using e-mail, you will probably find that it quickly becomes one of your main ways of communicating with family, friends and colleagues. The number of e-mails that you send and receive will increase substantially. Eventually, you will get to the stage where you need to sort your e-mails out – perhaps get rid of some, and organize others into folders. This is easily done – you just need to get yourself organized!

* You can organize your messages using the **Folders** list displayed on the left of the Inbox. You can toggle the display of the folders using the **Hide Folders/Show Folders** button in the Inbox.

To delete a message:

* Open the message and click **Delete** under the **Subject** field.

Or

1 Select the checkbox beside the message in the Inbox.

2 Click **Delete**.

* The deleted message is put in your Trash Can.

The Trash Can is emptied regularly (usually several times a week).

To recover a deleted message:

If you accidentally delete a message, you can recover it from the Trash Can (provided it hasn't been emptied).

1 Select the Trash Can folder (on the left side of your Inbox) to display its contents.

2 Select the checkbox by the message you wish to recover.

3 Choose a folder from the **Recover to Folder** list.

E-mail folders

If you receive a lot of e-mails from the same source, or about the same topic, you might want to organize the messages into folders so that you can find them easily.

To create a new folder:

1 Click **Create Folder** to open the **Create Folder** dialog box.

2 Give your folder a name.

3 Click **OK**.

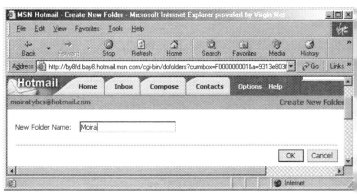

To move message to a folder:

1 Select the checkbox to the left of the message.

2 Click the drop-down arrow on the **Put in Folder...** list.

3 Select the folder that the message should move to.

To manage folders:

You can rename or delete any folders that you create.

1 Click **Manage Folders** in the Folders Pane.

2 Select the folder that you wish to rename or delete.

3 To rename the folder, click **Rename**, complete the dialog box and click **OK**.

Or

4 To delete the folder, click **Delete** and respond to the prompt that asks you to confirm the deletion or cancel.

* You can also create a folder from the **Manage Folders** dialog box.

Summary

In this chapter you have learnt how to:

* Access the Internet
* Locate a web site or page using a URL
* Specify your Home Page
* Save a web page to disk
* Use the Help system
* Change your toolbar display
* Display/hide images on a web page
* Use Hyperlinks to jump from one page to another
* Search the Web for sites and pages that may be of interest to you
* Add a URL to your Favorites
* Copy information from a web page into a file
* Print a web page
* Create and send e-mail messages
* Add details to the **To**, **cc** and **bcc** fields
* Read a message in your Inbox
* Add a signature to your message
* Cut/Copy and paste text from one message to another or from a different file into your e-mail message
* Read an attachment
* Reply to an e-mail message
* Attach a file to an e-mail message
* Add, delete and edit Contacts in Address Book
* Manage your messages

taking it further

Sound basic PC skills are useful on many different levels – personal, educational and vocational. Now that you have improved your PC skills, why not consider going for certification? The challenge of an exam can be fun, and a recognized certificate may improve your job prospects.

You might want to consider MOUS exams (Microsoft Office User Specialist) or ECDL (European Computer Driving Licence) or the SQA (Scottish Qualifications Authority) PC Passport (due to be launched in January 2004), or the new CLAIT exams.

Visit www.microsoft.com/traincert/mcp/mous/ for more on MOUS certification, www.ecdl.com for information on ECDL, www.sqa.org.uk for SQA certificates or www.new-clait.co.uk/ for CLAIT.

If you want to extend your knowledge of the software introduced in this book why not try the other Teach Yourself books in the series:

* *Teach Yourself Windows XP*
* *Teach Yourself Word*
* *Teach Yourself Excel*
* *Teach Yourself Access*
* *Teach Yourself PowerPoint*
* *Teach Yourself the Internet*

Wishing your every success with your PC!

index

teach yourself

Word 2002
moira stephen

- Are you new to Word?
- Do you want help with many of the topics commonly found in exam syllabuses?
- Do you need lots of practice and examples to brush up your skills?

Word 2002 is a comprehensive guide to this word processing package and is suitable for beginners. The book progresses from basic skills to more advanced features, with many time-saving shortcuts. Its practical approach, numerous illustrations and guide to automating tasks make it an easy way to brush up your skills.

Moira Stephen is a college lecturer and consultant trainer specializing in PC applications. She is the author of numerous computer books.